1917 – 2017
One Hundred Years of White Sox Baseball

Highlighting the Great 1917
World Series Championship Team

"The Greatest Franchise That Never Was!"

Go White Sox!

Mark Pienkos
7-8-2017

by
Mark Pienkos
with Foreword by Paul Ladewski

the **Peppertree Press**
Sarasota, Florida

Acknowledgements

This book is dedicated to all baseball diamond heroes past and present and the joy they brought and continue to bring to their loyal fans of this great game. It's also dedicated to the fans – especially those youngsters who played and continue to play the game in hopes of one time playing in the Big Leagues. These are the real heroes of the game of baseball. Especially, I dedicate this book to our family: wife, Ann, and our children - Michelle, Karen, and Stephen, plus our grandkids, Estelle, Amy, and Nathan. All heroes in my book, especially Nathan, who is our Superhero!

I wish to acknowledge my parents, Stella and Edward, who taught me more than baseball while growing up on the South Side of Chicago. The important values of religion, family, hard work, education, our Polish ethnic pride, and a constant belief that anything is possible was a constant drumbeat in our loving and supportive home.

I wish to acknowledge my two older brothers, Don and Ed, who were role models to me while growing up in the Windy City. They taught me many things including sportsmanship, fairness, and always to do your best, even in the face of overwhelming odds. Little did they know that allowing me to tag along with them while they played sports "with the big kids on the block" when we lived on

57th and Neva and later when we moved to 48th and Keeler in Chicago would give me the confidence to know that I could do anything I made up my mind to do.

I want to acknowledge my long-time friend Paul Ladewski who graciously agreed to write the Foreword for this book. Paul and I go way back to our high school days at St. Laurence High School in suburban Chicago. His sports journalism career is outstanding, but his friendship is even more so.

I am fortunate to have made many friends over the years – some who are baseball fans, some not. One who is a devoted fan of the game is Doug Callaghan, whose friendship has helped me appreciate his Tampa Bay Rays, as well as the fever spring training brings to those living in the Florida Gulf area. Another guy I must acknowledge is my first-year Resident Assistant at Northern Illinois University, Vic DiPrizio. I have never met a more devoted Chicago Cubs fan in my life. I am happy Vic could experience the exhilaration of his Cubbies winning the World Series in 2016. Now, we can both enjoy the satisfaction of seeing our favorite teams "winning it all" during our lifetimes. Thanks to six married couples who have stuck together with my wife and me since our Northern Illinois University days – Cathy & John Blozis, Anita & Greg Flanagan, Linda & Moon Mullen, Steph & Tony Scantlen, Linda & Tom Thunder, plus newbies Barbara & Mike Montes – Huskie Fans thru and thru. My A.I.O. "fraternity" brothers who I also bonded with at N.I.U. – aforementioned Paul Ladewski and his wife, Sharon, Vic & Pat DiPrizio, as well as Narch & Shawn Modesto, Gary & Becky Anderson, Jack & Nimfa Simpson, Mike Obarski and his soulmate Harriet. From my USC days and until now Barbara Hamilton and Rafe Trickey for their integrity. Also, my buddy, Joe

Lynch and his wife, Ann. Looking for a role model? Look no further than Mr. Lynch. What a beautiful human being – even though he's a Milwaukee Brewer fan. Speaking of Brewer fans, Sue and Jim Kandler are big boosters of mine. All these friends – too countless to mention – have enriched my life's journey.

Thank you to Julie Ann James, Publisher and Founder of the Peppertree Press in Sarasota for her support and guidance through the writing and publishing of this book. From day one, Julie Ann made sure that my book would reach the bookshelves. We hope you enjoy reading it!

Thank you to Teri Lynn Franco, Editorial Director at the Peppertree Press for her assistance in the publishing process as well as Becky Barbier for the book design.

A dedicated White Sox fan like me writing about his favorite team probably shouldn't quote a New York Yankee, but in this case, I think it's appropriate. Lou Gehrig said on July 4, 1939: "… Today I consider myself the luckiest man on the face of the earth." That's exactly how I feel to have married Ann nearly 45 years ago. She has been my North Star through the journey of life. Her support and love have meant the world to me. I hit a grand slam homer when I met Ann on her 16th birthday in 1966. Lucky me!

Photo courtesy of the National Baseball Hall of Fame and Library.

1917 Chicago White Sox
American League Champions
Season Record: 100 Wins 54 Losses

Row 1: Ziggy Hasbrouck, Lefty Williams, Shano Collins, Nemo Leibold, "Shoeless" Joe Jackson.

Row 2: Fred McMullin, Mellie Wolfgang, Joe Jenkins, Manager Clarence "Pants" Rowland, Eddie Cicotte, Byrd Lynn, Reb Russell, Happy Felsch.

Row 3: Eddie Collins, Buck Weaver, Eddie Murphy, Chick Gandil, Joe Benz, Ted Jourdan, Swede Risberg, Urban "Red" Faber.

1917 World Series

Game 1	Chicago White Sox 2	New York Giants 1
Game 2	Chicago White Sox 7	New York Giants 2
Game 3	New York Giants 2	Chicago White Sox 0
Game 4	New York Giants 5	Chicago White Sox 0
Game 5	Chicago White Sox 8	New York Giants 5
Game 6	Chicago White Sox 4	New York Giants 2

1917 — 2017
Chicago White Sox

"The Greatest Franchise That Never Was!"

Table of Contents

Foreword

By Paul Ladewski

Is there a more tortured, more savvy, more South Side tough person in all of baseball than a White Sox fan?

Say it ain't so, Joe. The damn Yankees. Swoontember of '67. Tito Freaking Landrum. Sosa for Bell. Bevington's reign of error. The strike of '94. Disappointments, White Sox fans got a million of 'em.

Through thin and thinner, though, White Sox fans always come back for more. They're more loyal than a wolf pack. They can find a silver lining in a botched squeeze bunt. They believe a 1-0 count is the start of a rally.

These people are so sick, they're funny, I tell ya.

See, I've known one in particular for a while now.

Mark and I met in high school. We talked ball at lunch tables. Competed in the driveway. Went to college together. Here it is a few million pitches later, and guess who's still hopeful about his Hosers?

Tell you something else about White Sox fans – they're real, not fake. No bandwagon-jumpers here.

White Sox fans like things in black and white, not color. They believe in basics, not curses, black cats and rotten luck. They can tell you the score – and the count, too. They don't just know good baseball. They demand it . . .

Tipton for Fox. The Go-Go Sox. The South Side Hit Men. Wilbur and Dick. The Big Hurt. Winnin' Ugly in '83. Winnin' it all in '05. Memories, White Sox fans got a million of those, too.

(Now should I tell them about that other team in town?)

Paul Ladewski is a sports columnist for the San Francisco Examiner and former sports editor, sportswriter and columnist for the Daily Southtown newspaper in Chicago. As a veteran member of the Baseball Writers Association, Paul is a Baseball Hall of Fame voter. Among his many honors, Paul was the recipient of the Peter Lisagor and Illinois Sports Columnist of the Year awards. In 2014, Paul was selected as the Executive Director for the Chicago Baseball Museum where he has also served as its website editor and correspondent. Paul and Mark became friends during their freshman year at St. Laurence High School in Burbank, Illinois. They also attended Northern Illinois University where they both graduated in 1972. Their friendship extends nearly fifty years!

*"My son John was born in the morning,
I aired a doubleheader in the afternoon,
and covered the fight that night."*

—Hal Totten

Hal Totten announcing White Sox games on WMAQ Radio in 1926. In 2016, Totten was one of ten finalists for the Ford C. Frick Award, presented annually for excellence in baseball broadcasting by the National Baseball Hall of Fame.

Chapter One

On Deck

A CENTURY – ONE HUNDRED YEARS – IS A LONG TIME

Let's assume no one is still alive who saw the World Series Champion Chicago White Sox play during the 1917 season. No one from that era is alive to tell the story of how great that 1917 team was. Certainly people over the years have written about some of its players. The most famous is "Shoeless" Joe Jackson whose life has been written about in books and portrayed in movies. One of these books is Eliot Asinof's *Eight Men Out* that details the story of the 1919 Black Sox scandal that saw eight players from the American League pennant-winning Chicago team conspire to throw the World Series against the Cincinnati Reds. I read this book when I was about thirteen or fourteen years old. My brother, Don, gave me a copy.

I remember devouring this book as the 1964 baseball season was about to begin. There were lots of discussions going on in the papers as *Chicago Tribune* and *Sun-Times* sports writers chronicled the prospects of the two Chicago teams – Cubs and Sox – as they got ready to start the season. Although there is still a pretty hefty rivalry between Sox and Cub fans, I think this has mellowed over the years. Not in my family, mind you; but I think it has just changed over time. In fact, today you occasionally hear

Chicagoans talk about hoping that both teams do well – or if my White Sox can't win the pennant (or World Series), I'll root for the Cubs. Not in my day! There was a rivalry that existed then and you were either a Sox or Cub fan, and as the saying goes, "Never the twain shall meet."

Asinof's book fascinated me as I began to realize how beautiful baseball history is. Certainly, baseball is about records and statistics, players and franchises, but *Eight Men Out* meant something more to me. It humanized the players. I got a chance to better understand that the players – especially the White Sox of 1919 – were more than just names. I learned about how great "Shoeless" Joe really was, plus I learned about third baseman Buck Weaver, centerfielder Happy Felsch and, of course, knuckleball pitcher Eddie Cicotte. Those four players in my estimation – Jackson, Weaver, Felsch, and Cicotte – were potential Hall of Famers; especially Jackson. This great hitter, fielder, and baserunner was already recognized by his fellow ballplayers, as well as by fans and sportswriters alike, as one of the premier stars in the game. Yet, the team was made up of other very interesting players, too. Players like Ray "Cracker" Schalk, "Cocky" Eddie Collins and Urban "Red" Faber who were later inducted into Cooperstown. The team also consisted of the other four "Black Sox": the ringleader of the World Series fix, first baseman Chick Gandil, shortstop Swede Risberg, utility infielder Fred McMullin, and pitcher Claude "Lefty" Williams. Of these four, Williams had the potential of being a Hall of Famer. All of these were members of the 1917 World Series champion team, too. So, of the eight players who would eventually be banned from baseball at the tail end of the 1920 season, at least five players had the potential – with Jackson being a certainty – for Hall of Fame consideration.

Asinof's description of the players and the 1919 World Series made me think of not only what happened, but what might have been as far as a Chicago White Sox dynasty. "What might have been" is always a question that surfaces when something interferes with what seems to be the normal scheme of things. In my young mind, I dreamed of "what might have been?" Could the fortunes of my Chicago White Sox been different had those eight players not gone over to the dark side? It's a question that has haunted me, as well as I believe many White Sox fans, over the years.

Fast-forward thirty years to 1989 when the movie *Field of Dreams* came to the big screen. Here was another reminder to me of "what might have been?" I saw a fictionalized recounting of old-time great baseball players walking out of an Iowa cornfield to play a game of baseball! One of those players was "Shoeless" Joe Jackson. The movie was a box-office sensation and considered to be one of the best baseball movies of all time. Many people - including our son, Steve, daughter, Karen, and me - drove to Dyersville, Iowa to see the field that was honed into a cornfield. Visitors, including ourselves on that special day, played a game of catch or ran the bases. But, for some it was even more. It brought to the forefront one of the greatest baseball players of all-time; a player who never achieved the ultimate recognition that he was justly due: Hall of Fame induction. For a time, there were revived efforts to extinguish this stain from Jackson's career and allow him entry. People began to do their own research on the Black Sox and a serious attempt was made to exonerate Buck Weaver from what had happened seventy years earlier. The reason? Weaver had not taken part in the throwing of the 1919 World Series, he simply had knowledge of it, yet never spoke up. In 1920, he was banned from baseball for life for not doing so. Jackson's defense was that he was illiterate; so how could he have signed a confession of his wrongdoing if he couldn't read it? Nonetheless, Jackson was banished from the game he loved for life, along with teammates mentioned above.

A potential dynasty on the South Side of Chicago never was allowed to take root.

That young Sox fan back in the early 1960s didn't really grasp what this all meant. But, reading and learning more about the White Sox through *Eight Men Out* helped me better understand what it meant to be a baseball fan. What it meant to show allegiance to your team. It helped cement a love of the game of baseball – and the Chicago White Sox – throughout my life. And, I have been grateful to have been able to share this love with our kids. It's a real joy to know that they love baseball, too! In their own ways, they will carry forward their experiences about a game that is very special.

Please enjoy my brief history of the 1917 White Sox team, as well as some highlights of its glorious past. *I also hope you will enjoy my personal vignettes of being a Chicago White Sox fan. You will find these interspersed throughout this book in italics.*

I also want to thank sources I consulted to put together this book. The first is *The Official Encyclopedia of Baseball,* 1963 Edition. I think it's the most read book by me during my lifetime. It was a book my Dad got as a freebie when he bought a box of White Owl cigars. He signed it "Stan Musial" and it took a little while before I realized it was my Dad's writing rather than the greatest Polish baseball player of all time. That's my Pops – playing another practical joke on me. The second is the 1979 edition of the same book. Finally, I extensively researched player stats and records using the following sources:

The Official Encyclopedia of Baseball
Hy Turkin and S.C. Thompson
(1963 Edition and Tenth Edition)

Eight Men Out
Eliot Asinof (1963)

The Ginger Kid: The Buck Weaver Story
Irving Stein (1992)

Chicago White Sox Official Website
whitesox.com

Major League Baseball Official Website
MLB.com

National Baseball Hall of Fame and Museum
baseballhall.org

Chicago Baseball Museum
chicagobaseballmuseum.org

Baseball Almanac
Baseball-almanac.com

Society for Baseball Research
sabr.org

Sports Reference, LLC
Baseball-Reference.com

This Great Game
thisgreatgame.com

Chicago Public Library
ChiPubLib.org

Chicago Sun-Times
chicago.suntimes.com

Chicago Tribune
chicagotribune.com
Wikipedia

Mayor of Chicago!

—Harry Creighton

Creighton was a popular broadcaster for the White Sox from 1949-1956. He frequently took over the play-by-play announcing from Jack Brickhouse. As a result, he was the original Harry to whom fans used to call when shouting "Hey, Harry" towards the broadcast booth.

It was once said that Creighton made so many appearances on television hawking products that he became more familiar to the public than the Mayor of Chicago.

1ˢᵗ Inning

To what extent would you go to see a baseball game?
Would you go so far as to quit your job?

That's exactly what I did in order to see a White Sox game – or as it turned out to be a long Sunday rain-delayed White Sox game!

Growing up on the South Side of Chicago, my first job was as a busboy at the Log Cabin Restaurant located on Archer Avenue near Keeler Avenue. It was a ten minute walk from our home to the restaurant as we lived at 48th and Keeler Avenue.

I was about 12 or 13 years old when I started working at this family restaurant which also served as a nice banquet facility for all sorts of occasions, including weddings, anniversaries, etc. As a busboy, my work involved basic duties such as preparing tables, scooping out and making butter balls for rolls and bread, pouring water, serving desserts, and cleaning up after meals. Basically, I assisted the wait staff in making sure our guests were given the best service possible. My recollection was that Log Cabin was a popular place for a quiet meal enjoyed by a couple or a large party of between 100 or 150 guests. I enjoyed working there for two-plus years during the school year and especially my summers. I think I made maybe $1.00 an hour, plus I received some of the tips shared between the *waitstaff and other busboys. My final few months of employment saw me graduate to stocking the bar. This task involved me counting the bottles of beer, wine, liquor, and other items for the bartender and then going to the basement storage area to get the items needed. Sometimes when we were in the midst of an event, the bartender would tell me to get a bottle of liquor because he was running low. I felt important as I was now doing additional duties because of the trust given to me by the owners.*

Overall, the owner Ollie, and his family were good to me and the other employees. But, between school, work, and summers playing baseball, the job didn't afford me many days off to go to a White Sox game – which I really wanted to do as I followed the team very closely by reading the daily newspaper and listening to games on the radio.

One summer week in 1964, I checked the baseball schedule for an upcoming weekend game that I might be able to squeeze in around my work and Little League games. I saw the Baltimore Orioles were coming to town and were going to play a weekend series. I started to focus on the Sunday, August 23 finale, which was also a double-header. One thing that I noticed was that the Sox were in the midst of a winning streak —they had just swept the Yankees in five games—which only got me more excited about going to a game. I mentioned my interest to go to the game to Ollie and wondered if I could have Sunday off. Everything appeared set for me to be able to go. I worked Friday night and Saturday afternoon and all of Saturday night. I went to church early on Sunday and headed off to work for a few hours before being able to leave to go to Comiskey Park. I was really looking forward to seeing the Sox play the Orioles, especially the possibility of seeing Sad Sam "Toothpick" Jones pitch in one of the games for the Orioles. I had heard of Jones and wanted to see him in action. One fact about Jones was that in 1955, as a member of the Chicago Cubs, he made Major League baseball history by being the first African-American pitcher to fire a no-hitter. The Pittsburgh Pirates were his victim in Wrigley Field.

As I left church and hustled off to Log Cabin, I wondered if the game would even be played that day. Chicago had been experiencing some weird weather for August. It was drizzling and the clouds didn't look like they were going to let up and it felt cool. When I arrived at work, I mentioned to Ollie about the fact that I worked on Friday and Saturday and that I was going to put in a few hours before hopping the Archer Avenue bus to go to the Sox game. Much to my surprise, he said I couldn't get the time off! What? I began pleading with Ollie to please let me go, but he wouldn't budge.

What a dilemma for a young person to be in. Do I stand my ground or give in, stay at work . . . and miss seeing my Sox play?

I quit! Right there on the spot . . . I quit!

Hey, you have to make tough choices in life and this was one of them. Loyalty to my employer or loyalty to my favorite pastime – baseball . . . and my beloved White Sox?

I left Log Cabin and never looked back. I hopped the Archer Avenue bus, got off at Rockwell and transferred to the 35th Street bus that headed to Comiskey. It drizzled parts of the day. I recall there was even a rain delay, but I stayed through it all hoping to see Sam Jones pitch. He didn't. The Sox lost the first game 7-3, but won the night-cap, 3-1. I finally got to see my Sox play. I arrived home around 7:30 p.m. after calling my Dad to pick me up at the ballpark. I was a little *soaked, tired, but at the same time happy that I had stood my ground and gone to the ballpark.*

By the way, leaving Log Cabin had another silver lining. A friend learned that I had quit my busboy job and he told me that a small factory – Ready Metals – located on 44th and Keating (where his father worked) was a place for me to consider working. I wasn't old enough to apply at that time, but I remembered my friend's recommendation. When I was in high school and turned sixteen, I applied for a $1.50 per hour summer job at Ready Metals. I got it and was able to continue working there part-time during the school year. That wasn't the only plus.

You see, about a year later, another high school buddy of mine, Mitch, told me of a girl's party that was going to be taking place on her 16th birthday, October 26, 1966. She lived two blocks from Ready Metals. I got myself invited and met the birthday girl, Ann. In fact, after ringing her parent's doorbell, Ann was the first person to greet me. Little did I know that we would begin a relationship that eventually turned into courtship and marriage on August 12, 1972. I like to tell people that "When Ann opened that door, she welcomed me into her life." Our life together has been a fabulous one. Not only have we enjoyed a great life together, we have three wonderful kids: Michelle, Karen, and Stephen. You won't find two more loyal Sox fans than Michelle and Steve. We're still working on Karen though! Her husband is a Milwaukee Brewers fan.

Vintage 1980 Chicago White Sox Painters Cap

"It's gone, good-bye."

"On Father's Day, we wish you all Happy Birthday."

"Solo homers usually come with no one on base."

"All of his saves have come in relief appearances."

"If Casey Stengel were alive today, he'd be spinning in his grave."

"We'll be back after this word from Manufacturer's Hangover."

—Ralph Kiner

Admitted into the Hall of Fame in 1975 as a player, Kiner spent his first year broadcasting White Sox games in 1961. His last year as an announcer was in 2004 for the New York Mets. A sensational player during his career, in the broadcast booth Kiner was known for his occasional malapropism that endeared him, once again, to fans.

Chapter Two

The Chicago White Sox: 1917–2017

"The Greatest Franchise That Never Was!"

When you think of baseball, the team that dominates the conversation is the New York Yankees. The Yankees actually began as a charter member of the American League in 1901, ironically as the Baltimore Orioles. In 1903, the club moved to New York and took the field as the New York Highlanders. It wasn't until 1913 that the greatest franchise in baseball history took the name New York Yankees.

Since 1913, the Yankees have dominated baseball winning 27 World Series titles, 40 American League pennants, 18 Eastern Division titles, and 4 Wild Card berths. It's an amazing story, especially when one takes a look at the next best franchises regarding winning titles. For example, the next three major league ball clubs with World Series appearances and rings are: the Giants (playing in New York and San Francisco) with 20 World Series appearances – winning 8 and losing 12; the St. Louis Cardinals with 18 World Series appearances – winning 11 and losing 7; and the Dodgers (playing in Brooklyn and Los Angeles) also with

18 World Series appearances – winning 6 and losing 12. Yes, the Yankees are the all-time champions of baseball. But, why?

To answer this question, one needs to take a long look back to what was happening at the turn of the century – the 20th century that is. Many might know it, but baseball's roots in America started in the late 1700s. But, the game as we know it had its beginnings in the 1870s. Various professional leagues started as the game evolved until the emergence of what we now call the National League was formed in 1876 and it wasn't until 1901 when the American League was founded.

The first World Series was played in 1903 when the Pittsburgh Pirates, winners of the National League pennant faced the American League champions, Boston Americans. Boston prevailed in a best-of-nine series, 5 games to 2. Interleague disputes prevented the playing of the World Series in 1904 which would have pitted the Boston Americans against the New York Giants. The World Series returned in 1905 when the New York Giants beat the Philadelphia A's in a seven game series, 4-1. Since then, the Fall Classic has been contested without interruption except for the 1994 season when a players' strike prevented the Series to be played.

During the early years of baseball, players were not paid much for their services, plus once players signed with a major league club they were in effect owned by the team. There was no free agency allowing players to have teams bid for their services as is the case today. Ballplayers in the early 1900's played the game for salaries that placed them above what the average citizen made, but at the same time they were forced to take what the owners would give them.

In this atmosphere, and with little oversight by a league commission that had the powers to enforce rules and regulations, some players took to betting on games to help boost their pay. Rumors began to float around the league that certain players were not playing the game as it was intended. Gamblers saw opportunities to make money on not only betting on the outcomes of games, but also enhancing their chances by bribing players to help determine the final score. The most famous of these betting scandals took place in the 1919 World Series when the Chicago White Sox, winners of the American League crown, took on the Cincinnati Reds in a best five out of nine World Series. The Whites Sox lost the series 5 games to 3 and many who watched the games wondered how the heavily favored White Sox could lose the World Series? Throughout the off-season and into the 1920 season, the rumors continued until finally charges were brought against eight White Sox players. Although they were ruled not guilty in court, the new commissioner of baseball, Judge Kennesaw Landis, immediately banned the players for life because of their involvement in the betting scandal.

Baseball now faced a credibility issue with its fans who wondered how up and up were the games they were paying good, hard-earned money to watch. Baseball needed a way to win the fans' trust back into the game and it came in the form of a bigger-than-life figure: George Herman Ruth, better known as the "Babe." Ruth had been purchased by the New York Yankees from the Boston Red Sox in 1919 for $100,000. Beginning in 1923, Ruth and his fellow Yankees began a run of 27 World Series championships. His enormous popularity, punctuated by his home run hitting prowess, brought fans to ballparks and renewed their interest and faith in the game of baseball. The New York Yankees became the preeminent franchise not only in baseball, but all of sports.

But, might this have all been different?

White Sox fans could argue that the mantle of dynasty should have been placed on their beloved team as they had arguably one of the finest teams ever assembled to compete in those early years of baseball. The 1919 World Series scandal gutted their team and excellent season they were enjoying in 1920 after Judge Landis issued his banishment of the seven Chicago players (one had retired after the 1919 season) for life. When the players were banned on September 26, the White Sox were just one half-game behind the Cleveland Indians. But, after the ban, the Sox went 2-2 to end the 1920 season two games behind the pennant winning Indians. The Sox never saw the first division of the American League again until 1936.

2017 marks the 100th anniversary of the 1917 World Series Champion Chicago White Sox. That team won a still team record 100 games. Their line-up was a mix of all-stars and potential Hall of Fame players. Led by "Shoeless" Joe Jackson, one of baseball's all-time players, both offensively and defensively, the White Sox certainly had the talent to be the premier baseball team not only in 1917, but also 1919, 1920 and beyond. They had the makings of a franchise that could have rivaled the accomplishments of the Yankees.

Since 1917, the White Sox have gone through some very lean years, winning the pennant in 1919 and then having to wait forty years to again return to the World Series. The 1959 "Go-Go" Sox team lost to the Los Angeles Dodgers 4 games to 2. Since 1959, the White Sox won the Western Division title in 1983 and 1993, and the Central Division title in 2000, 2005, and 2008. In 2005, the White Sox won their third World Series title having won previously in 1906 and 1917.

This book is written from the perspective of a life-long White Sox fan. Born in 1950, I've followed my team for the past 50 plus years. From attending my first baseball game at the old Comiskey Park in 1959 to the many seasons that followed, I've enjoyed – and at times suffered the same frustrations that baseball fans experience as they follow their team through the long seasons of baseball. Hope springs eternal each opening day of the baseball season as fans hope for the best based on predictions, off-season trades and player acquisitions. The hot stove league each winter provides many opportunities for fans to dream of what is to come as the first pitch of the season takes place. Unfortunately, hopes are often dashed by the reality that each day brings on the field. Losses outnumber wins and the long-hoped for season of success drifts into another "what might have been" winter of hope for the next season.

Throughout my life, I've seen my own share of disappointments and frustrations as my White Sox either failed to play up to their potential or simply weren't really good enough to compete for the coveted World Series ring. But, that never stops a true fan from believing that "this year" will be "the year" when a championship will be the reward after a long baseball season.

However, I would be remiss if I didn't also say that I've had plenty of joys watching my White Sox play exciting games, or watching a new prospect don the Chicago uniform worn by my South Side heroes, or hoping that a veteran player would have just one more career year left in his bat or pitching arm. Yes, the fun of baseball is watching a game that is filled with history, as well as wonderful memories of years gone by. It includes your dad taking you to your first ballgame, or seeing the vast baseball field for the first time, or remembering where you were when something special happened on the field of your favorite team. What baseball fan can't recall his or her favorite baseball player – his uniform number, position on the field, batting/pitching statistics, or his Bazooka Bubble Gum baseball card?

This book chronicles a great franchise. More importantly, it includes some personal vignettes about a kid growing up on the South Side of Chicago and learning not only about his beloved White Sox, but also about the great game of baseball. Finally, as every childhood rolls into adulthood, how that "kid" continues his love of the game while also sharing its wonderful grandeur and history with his own children.

What might have been had the "Black Sox" players of 1919 not traded their own love of the game for whatever they were looking for: money, revenge for being paid less than what they thought they were worth, or just simply doing things they felt other players were doing? We will never know if the Chicago White Sox team of the Roaring Twenties might have equaled or surpassed the Yankees, but this kid believes baseball history might have been different.

In the pages that follow, I hope Chicago White Sox fans will revel in that great World Series team of 1917. I also hope that fans of other teams will gain a greater appreciation of that team from 100 years ago that excited baseball fans around the nation. Learning about the players of not only that championship season, but also players and highlights of the many seasons that followed are chronicled here. Enjoy my own ruminations of what it has meant to be a loyal White Sox fan. Whether you are a Sox fan, or a fan of another baseball team, I know you will take a moment to think back about your own baseball memories.

Our family has established an educational fund to grant scholarships for students. It's called the Stella and Edward Pienkos Educational Fund. A portion of the proceeds from this book goes to this scholarship fund. So, besides getting enjoyment from either reading this book or giving it to someone as a gift, you are also helping to support a young person in their pursuit of their own education . . . and future.

I hear the umpire yelling "Play Ball!" so let's get on with the story of the "Greatest Franchise that Never Was" – the Chicago White Sox!

"Holy Mackerel!"

—Vince Lloyd

Long-time Chicago sportscaster who broadcast White Sox games from 1955-1964. Well-known for his deep voice, Lloyd's broadcast career lasted over thirty years. Among his many accomplishments, Lloyd was the first sports announcer to interview a sitting United States President. This occurred in pre-game festivities prior to the White Sox opener versus the host Washington Senators in 1961 when he interviewed John F. Kennedy. Although very deserving, Lloyd has not received the Ford C. Frick Award for broadcasters sponsored annually by the National Baseball Hall of Fame. Hopefully, this omission will eventually be corrected.

2nd Inning

FIRST EXPERIENCE AT A BALLGAME

Talk to any baseball fan and they can usually bend your ear as to their first experience at a Major League baseball game. For many, it begins the long journey of falling in love with the game.

For me, that love affair has lasted nearly 60 years!

Although I listened on the radio to many games growing up in Chicago, I vividly remember my first game at the ballpark. My dad took my two older brothers and me to a weeknight game at old Comiskey Park during the summer of 1959. The White Sox were hosting the Boston Red Sox with the great number 9, Ted Williams, leading the Bosox.

Of course, my Chisox had the best ballplayers ever to grace the field! And little did I know that this 1959 White Sox team would win the American League pennant and play in its first World Series since 1919.

My dad got home from his job at Crane Company around 4:00 p.m. and after a light supper, we all headed down to 35th and Shields for the game. I'm not sure how many games my brothers Ed or Don had gone to in their lifetime, but this was going to be my first and I was very excited.

When we got to the game I was once again reminded of my dad's frugality as he parked on a side street near the park so we didn't have *to pay for parking. My dad was a factory worker who worked hard for the $2.00 an hour he made so he didn't take too kindly about having to pay for parking. This wasn't the only time we'd look for free parking rather than paying for a spot in a lot. As dad would say, "You can buy a couple of boxes of popcorn at the ballgame for the cost of paying to park." Strange, but that philosophy still remains with me today – and our three kids. When going out, we'll scour side streets for free parking rather than paying for it. Thanks, Dad.*

There was a great deal of excitement as we approached Comiskey. It seemed as if we'd never get through the ticket turnstiles. As we gave our tickets to the fellow at the gate, I remember all sorts of people scurrying around. Some were looking for the right tunnel or walkway to get to their seats while others were standing in line to buy a game program, hot dog, soda, or beer from a concession stand. I remember the noise, the chatter, and the smells of different foods being prepared for waiting fans.

As we walked to the upper deck level on the first base side of the field, I was anxious to get my first glimpse of what I had only dreamed about – the baseball diamond.

As I said earlier, most everyone recalls their first experience at a ballgame and I am no different. I still remember walking from the dimly lit tunnel out into the fresh early evening air. The lights were gleaming! The grass was glistening! I couldn't believe how big the field and ballpark was! I tried to take it all in as we tried to find our seats: The players warming up, the scoreboard, marveling at the lights, watching all the people moving about either in the aisles or in their seats.

It was a great experience and the first pitch hadn't even been thrown! One that I have never forgotten. As for the game itself, I remember Louie Apparicio reaching first base in the home half of the first inning and almost immediately the chant of "Go-Go-Go" rising up from the fans. For this was the '59 Go- Go White Sox that could take a walk by Little Louie, a bunt by second baseman Nellie Fox and a single by centerfielder Jim Landis or leftfielder Al Smith to manufacture a run. They did it all season and eventually to the pennant and their first World Series in forty years.

My brother, Ed, also had a great memory from my first game at Comiskey Park. He was able to scramble after a foul ball hit off the bat of a Red Sox player. And, yes, my dad made good on his promise to buy us all popcorn and a soda! I think my dad knew that this was a special day for me and he wanted to make sure I'd remember it. And I have!

"There's a shot . . . AND A GOAL!!!"

—Lloyd Petit

From 1965-1967, Petit was a Chicago sportscaster who broadcast White Sox games. In 1986, Petit received the Foster Hewitt Memorial Award — for outstanding contributions to the broadcasting profession and the game of hockey — by the Hockey Hall of Fame. There's a shot... AND A GOAL!!!" is his signature call announcing Chicago Blackhawk hockey games.

Chapter Three

THE 1917 Season!

The 1917 regular season for Chicago culminated in the White Sox bringing home their second World Series championship. Their first was a memorable one, too, besting their crosstown rival Cubs four games to two in the 1906 World Series. That Series was also special in that the Cubs had won 116 games and were considered the overwhelming favorites versus the White Sox. The Sox had a solid season themselves winning 93 games while dropping 58. However, their team batting average of .230 was the worst in the American League. Yet, the White Sox bested the Cubs in the first World Series contested between two teams from the same city. This is the first and only time this has happened in Chicago. Two other cities share bragging rights to this rare occurrence: New York in 1944 when the Brooklyn Dodgers took on the New York Yankees and in 1989 when the San Francisco Giants traveled back-and-forth across San Francisco Bay to face the Oakland Athletics. What made the Sox upset of the Cubs in 1906 so amazing was that the South Siders had the worst batting average in the American League. As a result, that Sox team was forever known as the "Hitless Wonders" for beating the Cubs in the World Series.

Of course, besides the two World Series championships the Sox won in 1906 and 1917, they also achieved a third in 2005. Their loyal fans had to wait an unbelievable eighty-eight years to finally see the ultimate baseball trophy brought back to the South Side of Chicago. But, that's a story for another chapter in this book.

Examining closely the 1917 season, there are several highlights, but as is the case in baseball, it's expected that the long season will have its ups and downs. Obviously, when you win 100 games as the Sox did that season, there were far more ups than downs. What I tried to do was break up the season into more or less three parts: the first fifty games, the second fifty games, and the final fifty games. By doing this, one can see how the Sox achieved their record-setting season of winning 100 games.

The 1917 campaign began with a road victory against the St. Louis Browns. After losing the next game, the Sox went on a tear winning eight of their next nine games. Their 9-2 record took a nose-dive over the next ten games seeing them win only twice while dropping eight games. Their record was an average one at that point of the season. Having played twenty-one games, the Sox record stood at 11-10, certainly not the makings of a championship season - let alone a record-breaking one. However, during the next 30 games (one of which ended in a tie), the White Sox would start their run towards greatness. Starting on May 8, once again against the Browns in St. Louis, the Sox would win twenty-two of their next twenty-nine games. Their record stood at 33-17. After fifty games, they were beginning to build a won-loss record that would lead them to being forty-six games over .500. During that first fifty game stretch, the Sox had several winning streaks: three 3 game win streaks, three 4 game win streaks, and one 8 game win streak. Also, the Sox never experienced any prolonged losing streaks. In fact, they had only one losing streak of four games, and one other losing streak of three games. They were playing consistent ball and in first place. During those first fifty games, the Sox had outscored their opponents 195-118! No wonder their pitching staff would have such a fine team ERA with mound ace Eddie Cicotte leading the league in that category.

The second third of the 1917 season began promisingly with Chicago beating the Red Sox in Boston, 8-0 and 7-2, before dropping the final two games of the four game series. During that fifty game middle portion of the season – that portion of the season that always tends to separate the average to the superlative teams – the Sox continued their winning ways going eight games over .500. On August 2, after 102 games played, their record reached the 63-37-2 mark (with two games ending in ties). Once again, the Sox played very consistent baseball with two 3 game win streaks, as well as three 4 game win streaks. They only experienced two losing streaks of any importance, one of three games beginning on July 5 against the Tigers in Detroit where they dropped the final two games of a five game series and then the first game of a four game set at home against the Philadelphia Athletics.

The White Sox were driving towards the end of the season. And did they ever start speeding during that final third of the campaign.

The final portion of the year – 54 games – saw the White Sox win twenty more games than they lost going 37-17 to finish with a franchise-record 100 wins and 54 losses! During that unbelievable stretch of games, the White Sox had only one 3 game losing streak and two 2 game losing streaks! Even more impressive was the fact that the White Sox had two 9 game winning streaks, plus two 3 game winning streaks! This was a team on a tear and there was no stopping them. They were not only determined to win the American League pennant, but also continue their dominance into the World Series – whoever was their opponent.

The White Sox compiled their 100 victories by winning decisively at home going 56-21 at Comiskey Park (.727 percentage) and 44-33 on the road (.571 percentage). During the entire season, the White Sox never experienced a losing month of baseball. They played .700 ball during the months of August and September. They dominated every team in the American League playing above .500 against all of the other seven teams. They played in 33 shutout games winning 22 of them. The Sox won 31 of the 55 one-run games they played in. This was a solid team that ran away with the American League crown and second place Boston Red Sox by nine games. The other first division teams were the third place Cleveland Indians (12 games back), and the Detroit Tigers (21½ games behind the White Sox). The second division of the eight team American League found the Washington Senators (25½ out of first place), the New York Yankees (28½ games behind), the St. Louis Browns (43 games back), and the cellar-dwelling Philadelphia Athletics (44½ games back of the White Sox).

The 1917 Chicago White Sox team had made a statement: They were a team to be reckoned with – not only during the upcoming World Series, but also for future seasons.

However, the future could wait. The Sox had a date with the National League pennant winner, New York Giants.

"Hardy on second,
Piersall on first, and dangerous
Vic Power is up ... one out.
Power ... is 1 for 4, an infield single
.... There's a ground ball ... Aparicio
has it ... steps on second,
throws to first ...
The Ball Game's over!
The White Sox are the
Champions of 1959!
A forty year ... wait has now ended!"

—Jack Brickhouse

Long-time sports announcer that included White Sox games on radio and TV. Brickhouse's career spanned five decades covering most every type of sporting event including baseball, football, basketball, boxing, and wrestling. Brickhouse also mastered assignments that took him to political conventions, as well as being a talk show host. He is best known for his home run call: "Back, back, back ... Hey! Hey!" Brickhouse earned entrance into the National Baseball Hall of Fame in 1983.

3rd Inning

1959 – Forty Years of Being 'An Also Ran'
Ends With Sirens Blaring!

Forty years is a long time, especially for a baseball fan looking forward to his or her team getting into the World Series. But, that's just what it was for Sox fans. From the infamous 1919 season until 1959, White Sox fans had to endure some pretty dismal seasons. During that forty-year span, the Sox made the first division (ending a season in one of the top four spots in the eight team American League granted you "first division" status) only sixteen times. If you look at the thirty-year period from 1919 to 1949, the Sox made the first division only eight times! Talk about a fan base that must have been very, very frustrated, as well as very patient for a winner. Those were pretty lean years for the Pale Hose. Fortunately, during the ten-year period from 1950-1959, the White Sox saw a resurgence as the team finished consistently high in the American League standings. During that stretch, they finished fourth one year (1951), third, five straight years (1952, 1953, 1954, 1955, and 1956), and second, twice (1957 and 1958). In 1959, Chicago finally won the American League pennant!

The hopes of that 1919 White Sox team, loaded with talent and the prospects of winning pennants and World Series Championships were

dashed by the Black Sox scandal. What might have been is only con-
jecture, but the results of the scandal had a devastating effect on team
records during the four decades that ensued.

The 1950s brought a resurgence of hope on the South Side. With
players being acquired by a shrewd baseball-savvy General Manager,
Frank Lane, the White Sox began to develop teams that not only
brought respectability in the won-loss column, but also gave Sox fans
hope that the White Sox would contend for an American League pennant! Lane was never shy of making trades and as a result earned the
nicknames of "Trader Frank," "Trader Lane" and "Frantic Frank."
As a result, the Sox began their consistent rise in the standings going
81-73 (3rd place in the American League) in 1952, 89-65 (3rd place)
in 1953, 94-60 (3rd place) in 1954, 91-63 (3rd place) in 1955, and
85-69 (3rd place) in 1956.

The hiring of Al Lopez as White Sox manager the following
season played an important role in this hope that a title was on the
horizon.

Lopez, better known as Senōr Lopez, eventually was named to the
Hall of Fame as a manager in 1977. However, he was an accomplished
catcher in his playing days, setting the record for most games played at
that position at 1,918 games. The record was broken by Bob Boone in
1987. Later, Carlton Fisk playing for the White Sox, set the record for
most games caught in 1993 at 2,226 games. Ivan Rodriquez broke
Fisk's record in 2009. Lopez also gained Hall of Fame immortality because of his skills as a manager. The Yankees continued to dominate the
American League in the 40s and 50s winning five consecutive World
Series Championships from 1948-1953. Lopez put a halt to that string
by managing the Cleveland Indians to the A.L. pennant in 1954 with
a 111-43 record, an American League record for season wins that stood
for 44 years. His team ran into a buzz saw in the World Series getting

On the morning of September 23, 1959, the *Chicago Tribune* proclaims the White Sox Champions of the American League! Sirens blare . . . and scare! On the road the night before, the White Sox defeated the Cleveland Indians, 4-2, in dramatic fashion killing a Tribe rally with a double play to end the game. The White Sox claimed their first title after a forty-year drought.

swept by the Willie Mays-led New York Giants, 4-0. But, Lopez had gained the attention of baseball insiders as a very skillful manager who got the most out of his players while using heady strategy. The Sox were becoming a well-respected team in the eyes of Sox fans.

Lopez was lured away from Cleveland in 1957 to take the helm of the White Sox. This was a stroke of genius by owner Charles Comiskey II and General Manager John Rigney. With talented players acquired by Comiskey and Rigney, and when ownership changed in 1959, Bill Veeck brought in Hank Greenberg as G.M. Lopez molded his team to become serious pennant-contenders in 1957, winning 90 games and finishing in second place, 1and in 1958, winning 82 games, again ending up in second place. The Yankees were still the dominant team, but Chicago was right on their heels.

1959 was a special year! Playing with a nucleus of solid players, the Sox parlayed excellent defense, timely hitting, formidable pitching, and overall team speed to achieve what no other White Sox team had accomplished since 1919: Win the American League pennant!

I listened to most every game I could on my transistor radio sometimes long into the middle of the night even on school nights. My Dad did, too, as did others in my neighborhood on 48th and Keeler. Many hot summer nights were spent on the back porch listening to announcer Bob "The Commander" Elson describe to his listeners about a play happening on the field. Elson had a signature voice, as well as the old school way of calling the game: sharp and concise. "Ground ball to second, Fox picks it up and throws to first, out by 20 feet." Or, "Ground ball to short, Aparicio has it, throws to first, out by 15 steps." How about a double play call? "Ground ball to Phillips at third, over to second for one, over to first for two, double play." Or, when a Sox player would hit a home run, Elson would say, "There's a long one to left by Lollar, it's a White Owl wallop by Sherm!" Elson would weave sponsors into his call of the game whether it was sponsors like White Owl cigars or Hamm's Beer. He must have been successful at hawking products because I remember my Dad puffing on White Owls and occasionally having a cool Hamm's beer after a hard day's work. Fans wanted to know what was happening on the field and Elson's style was to deliver a picture of just that. He didn't get into a lot of extraneous banter. Announcers were less in manufacturing enter-tainment rather wanting to let listeners know what was going on in the field. Elson was a master at painting a picture of baseball games to his listeners. Elson did play-by-play for the Sox from 1929 to 1970. In 1979, Elson received the Ford Frick Award and was elected to the Baseball Hall of Fame as a broadcaster. The Sox line-up in 1959 still sticks in my memory: Louie Aparicio leading off at shortstop, Nellie Fox at second base, Jim Landis in centerfield, Al Smith in left field, batting clean-up, Sherm Lollar catching, Bubba Phillips at third, Earl Torgeson at first base (and later Ted Kluzewski,), Jim McAnany and Jungle Jim Riviera shar-ing rightfield duties, and then batting ninth. a bevy of outstanding pitcher: southpaw Billy Pierce, right-handers Early "Gus" Wynn, Dick Donavan, Barry Latman, and Bob Shaw.

The Sox had an excellent bench with Sammy Esposito (No. 14) who would play variety of infield positions. Billy Goodman, (No. 6) also played a key role in support of the starters.

Relief pitching was impressive with Turk Lown and Gerry Staley being the workhorses in the late innings.

The entire regular season roster for the White Sox was:

#3 Jim McAnany	*#18 Barry Latman*
#4 Ron Jackson	*#19 Billy Pierce*
#5 Bubba Phillipos	*#20 Johnny Romano*
#6 Billy Goodman	*#21 Gerry Staley*
#7 Jim Rivera	*#22 Dick Donovan*
#8 Harry Simpson	*#24 Early Wynn*
#8 Ted Kluzewski	*#26 Earl Battey*
#9 Johnny Callison	*#27 Turk Lown*
#10 Sherman Lollar	*#29 Ray Moore*
#11 Louie Aparicio	*#32 Larry Doby*
#12 Gary Peters	*#32 J.C. Martin*
#14 Sammy Esposito	*#35 Bob Shaw*
#15 Ken McBride	*#38 Norm Cash*
#16 Al Smith	*#44 Cam Carreon*
#17 Earl Torgeson	

The mid-season acquisition of Ted "Big Klu" Kluzewski from the Cincinnati Reds put the finishing touches to a team that was poised for an exciting pennant run.

No Sox fan, or for that matter anyone living in Chicago will ever forget the night of Tuesday, September 22nd. That was the night the Sox clinched the pennant in a 4-2 thrilling victory over the Cleveland Indians. The Sox had taken over first place in late July, but the Indians hung around until that late September night. With one out in the bottom of the ninth, Gerry Staley forced Cleveland's Vic Power to hit into a double play to end the game, clinch the pennant, and end forty years of frustration. Watching on WGN TV, I remember Jack Brickhouse's call: "Hardy on second, Piersall on first, and dangerous Vic Power is up... one out. Power ...is 1 for 4

Baseball cards featuring 1959 White Sox players. What a team! What memories!

an infield single. There's a ground ball...Aparicio has it...steps on second, throws to first...the ball game's over! The White Sox are the Champions of 1959! A forty year... wait has now ended! What followed was something out of a Jules Verne science fiction novel.

Mayor Richard J. Daley, a big White Sox fan who grew up on the South Side of Chicago in the Bridgeport neighborhood, gave orders to sound air-raid sirens all across the city to celebrate the Sox winning the pennant!

Remember, in 1959 the U.S. was in the midst of the Cold War with the old Soviet Union. Both nations had nuclear missile arsenals that had the ability to obliterate the entire world. In schools, we practiced air-raid drills, people built bomb shelters, there were public broadcast announcements as to what to do in the event of a nuclear attack. These were scary times. So, when Mayor Daley ordered those air-raid sirens to blare across the Chicagoland area, it was an eerie sound to behold. For Sox fans, we were celebrating. For others who weren't following the baseball races it must have felt as if the world was coming to an end!

The 1959 American League pennant winners were to play in their first World Series in 40 years against the Los Angeles Dodgers who had deserted Brooklyn for the west coast in 1957. In their second season in L.A., the Dodgers reached the World Series.

Playing in the Los Angeles Coliseum, a massive stadium designed for the 1932 Olympics and for football, the Dodgers won the National League pennant with a team consisting of stars Duke Snider, Gil Hodges, Johnny Roseboro, Frank Howard, Don Drysdale, and Johnny Podres. There was even a southpaw named Sandy Koufax who was only beginning to assert himself as the dominant pitcher he would eventually become. But, it was lesser name players who made the biggest impact in the 1959 World Series. Second baseman Charlie Neal and utility man Chuck Essegian ruined the party for Chicago fans. The Dodgers won the World Series four games to two – with Larry Sherry starring in relief. Yet, the Sox made a Series of it throughout those six games.

The forty year drought to return to the World Series was over. Also, 1959 culminated a decade of very competitive White Sox teams that continually knocked on the American League pennant door. New York was their nemesis. Those darn Yankees were the nemesis of all of baseball!

Interestingly, after 1959, it would be an even longer wait for the White Sox to return to the World Series. However, the city of Chicago and its White Sox fans would celebrate a World Series Champion in 2005!

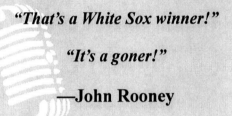

"That's a White Sox winner!"

"It's a goner!"

—**John Rooney**

Rooney spent eighteen years in the White Sox broadcast booth from 1988-2005. His final game broadcasting for the White Sox was on October 26, 2005 when he announced the final game of the White Sox World Series sweep of the Houston Astros. The following year, Rooney earned the distinction of being the only broadcaster to call consecutive championship seasons for two different ballclubs when he was in the broadcast booth announcing the St. Louis Cardinals World Series win over the Detroit Tigers.

Chapter Four

1917 World Series

New York Giants vs.
Chicago White Sox

Winning the 1917 regular season with a franchise record 100 games was a tremendous White Sox accomplishment. However, that wasn't the end of their storybook year. Here's a synopsis of the World Series. It was a fantastic six game Series, especially the finale in New York.

The 1917 National League pennant-winning New York Giants had a fine season in their own right. They won 98 games and lost 56 games under manager John McGraw, who would become one of the great skippers in baseball history and eventually inducted into the Hall of Fame.

Game 1
Comiskey Park, Chicago

The seven game World Series opened up in Chicago on October 6, 1917. The White Sox welcomed 32,000 fans as they jammed into Comiskey Park. White Sox ace Eddie Cicotte took the mound featuring his knuckleball, plus his league-leading 28-12 record, his league-best 1.53 ERA, and most innings pitched in the American League (346.2). His opponent was the Giants' Slim Sallee. In 1917, Sallee also had a fine season in his own right posting an 18-7 record. Cicotte and Sallee dueled the entire game, both pitching complete games with the White Sox besting the Giants 2-1. The difference in the Sox win was a fourth inning solo home run by centerfielder Happy Felsch.

Game 2
Comiskey Park, Chicago

Game two was played the next day and featured another Chicago stalwart, Urban "Red" Faber. Faber had a solid 1917 season posting a 16-13 won-loss record. In his fourth season with the White Sox, Faber was beginning to distinguish himself as one of the premier right-handed pitchers in baseball. In fact, Faber would spend his entire twenty-year career with the South Siders and during those many seasons, accumulated 254 wins while dropping 213 games. Unfortunately for Faber, he would pitch many a season with a second division ball club that was decimated as a result of the 1919 Black Sox scandal.

Yet, Faber would rise to the occasion in the 1917 World Series and, as a result, begin composing his own Hall of Fame resume.

Faber's mound opponent in Game 2 was Ferdie Schupp, who also had a strong 1917 campaign hurling for the Giants.

His 21-7 record was the best of his ten-year career scattered among four different teams that included the Giants, St. Louis Cardinals, Brooklyn Robins, and ironically, Chicago White Sox where he ended his career in 1922 posting a 4-4 record. But, on this October Sunday afternoon, Schupp would last only into the second inning after the White Sox tied the Giants 2-2. Relieving him was veteran right-hander Fred Anderson, who gave up four of the five runs the Sox erupted for in the home half of the fourth inning. That was enough for the White Sox to cruise to an easy 7-2 victory before another sellout crowd at Comiskey Park. Faber was the beneficiary of a Sox attack that featured 14 hits. Buck Weaver and Joe Jackson each had three hits as the White Sox took a 2-0 lead in the Series.

Game 3
Polo Grounds, New York

The 1917 World Series shifted cities and with it some momentum for the underdog Giants. The Polo Grounds in New York was the scene of the third game and over 33,000 loyal fans were on hand to try to get their hometown Giants in the win column. On the mound for the White Sox was first game winner Eddie Cicotte who this time faced Rube Benton. Benton's fine fifteen-year career was shared between the Cincinnati Reds and New York Giants and during those years he won 150 games while losing 144. Benton took his home field mound on Wednesday, October 10, 1917 and did what his manager, John McGraw, wanted him to do: duel White Sox ace Cicotte and beat him.

And that's just what Benton went out and did, shutting down the White Sox 2-0, yielding only five hits. Benton was helped by a three hit game, including a triple that led to a run, by outfielder Dave Robertson. Both Cicotte and Benton went the distance as the Giants shaved the Series lead, two games to one.

Game 4
Polo Grounds, New York

Game four was played the following day and saw the Giants even the Series at two games apiece. The potent White Sox lineup found itself stifled by game one starter, Ferdie Schupp, who scattered seven hits while going the route, winning 5-0. Schupp may have had trouble in his first appearance, but not this time. His mound opponent was World Series Game 2 winner, "Red" Faber. But, Faber was not as sharp, allowing three runs and seven hits over seven innings pitched. In addition, Giants centerfielder Bennie Kauff belted two home runs. The Series was now even at two games apiece and both teams had visions of taking the Series.

However, first would come the pivotal fifth games.

Game 5
Comiskey Park, Chicago

The scene of the Series shifted back to Chicago on Saturday, October 13th. With temperatures hovering around the high forties, a smaller crowd of 27,323 was on hand to see if their hometown baseball heroes could regain the edge in the Series. Game 5 starters were Ferdie

Sallee for the Giants and southpaw Reb Russell for the White Sox. Russell had posted a fine 15-5 record during the 1917 campaign and Manager "Pants" Rowland had confidence starting him in this important game. Rowland's confidence was quickly dashed. The Sox ran into immediate trouble in the first inning as New York scored two runs off Russell on two hits and a walk. Rowland decided to yank Russell for the experienced Cicotte with hopes of shutting down the Giants before the score got out of hand. Cicotte responded.

Cicotte kept the Sox in the game over the six innings he pitched in relief. Although he gave up two runs, "Knuckles" gave the White Sox time to regroup as they focused on rallying to take this important Game 5 of the World Series. Could they do it?

The Sox did score a run in the home half of the sixth inning to cut the Giants lead to 4-2. Relieving Cicotte in the top of the seventh was "Lefty" Williams who struck out the side in his one inning of relief, but allowed a run to score making it 5-2 going into the bottom of the seventh inning.

The Sox rallied in their time at-bat scoring three runs to tie the score at 5-5. Rowland once again went to his bullpen, this time asking "Red" Faber to hold New York while hoping his White Sox team could rally for more runs. Faber did just that toiling two scoreless innings while the Sox offense did their part scoring three runs in the bottom of the eighth. The Sox held on for an 8-5 victory and the Series lead, three games to two. Faber had won his second World Series victory.

Game 6
Polo Grounds, New York

Once again, the 1917 Series shifted back to New York with Game 6 being played on Monday, October 15th. Having confidence in his Game 5 winner, Urban Faber, White Sox Manager Rowland asked his right-hander to take the hill in the Polo Grounds. Nearly 34,000 fans were on hand to see if their hometown Giants could force a Game 7 in Chicago. Giants' Game 3 winner, Rube Benton, took to the mound and although pitched well at times, struggled to keep the potent White Sox line-up in check. Benton left the game after five innings having given up three unearned runs. He rightfully could blame the defense for his demise as two costly errors opened the floodgates in the White Sox top half of the fourth inning. A throwing error, a dropped fly-ball, and the failure of any Giant to cover home plate in a rundown between third and home after Eddie Collins eluded a tag by Giants' catcher, Bill Rariden, allowed the fleet-footed Collins to score the third run in the inning. Although New York rallied in the bottom of the fifth scoring two runs, cutting the Sox lead to 3-2, right-hander Pol Perritt yielded another run in his four innings of relief. Faber did not as he scattered six New York hits and the White Sox grabbed their second World Series Championship winning Game 6 by the score of 4-2. Faber was truly the World Series hero as he won three games and lost one in four appearances.

White Sox fans could rightfully celebrate not only their record-setting regular season team, but also winning the 1917

World Series! The White Sox claimed their second World Series title! Owner Charles Comiskey had once again brought Chicago White Sox fans a winner. Unfortunately, it would be another 88 years before the trophy would once again be hoisted high on the South Side of Chicago.

"Holy Toledo, what a play!"

Milo Hamilton

White Sox broadcaster from 1961-1965. During his sixty-year career, Hamilton broadcast games for the St. Louis Browns, St. Louis Cardinals, Chicago Cubs, Chicago White Sox, Atlanta Braves, Pittsburgh Pirates, and Houston Astros. In 1962, Hamilton received the Ford C. Frick Award and was admitted into the National Baseball Hall of Fame as a broadcaster.

4th Inning

THE NIGHT THE LIGHTS WENT OUT
AT COMISKEY

Growing up in Chicago, I did what many did – played lots of baseball!
Summers were filled with pick-up games – whether they be hard ball or
16" softball. We also played lots and lots of "fast pitching" which usu-
ally featured one player facing another using a dime rubber ball. Using
chalk, we would draw a strike zone on a playground wall. In my case,
Edwards School on 48th and Karlov provided my baseball diamond for
many of my summers in the '60s. "Fast pitch" was a way to play a game
with a minimum of people. One guy would pitch while the opponent
would bat. If you had more than one player on a team, the other person
played the field and took turns when it was your time to bat. The neat
thing about "fast-pitching" was that you could even play a game by your-
self. You just pitched a game against the wall and kept track of strikes
and balls and how many runs scored when your imaginary opponent got
walks. It felt like I must have pitched a million innings each summer!

Hours and hours were spent during the summer often from nine in
the morning until seven in the evening with the usual break between
games to head home for a bite to eat.

I played Little League for two years when I was growing up that just added to my time playing baseball. Besides games, there were practices to attend. You ate and slept baseball for those three months of summer.

I was a pretty good second baseman and outfielder, but met my match at the plate trying to get the bat on the ball. My first love was catching, but my parents nixed that idea because they thought I would get hurt. I remember crying and crying because I really wanted to be a catcher – the mitt, the chest protector, the shin guards, the catcher's mask, and, oh yes, the protective cup! I remember running around the house exclaiming, "I want my cup, I want my cup!" My brother, Ed, got sick of my yelling and got a sock and coffee mug tied them together and told me, "Here's your cup, now shut up already!"

I loved playing second base.

As Little Leaguers, we got to dress up and marched in the Memorial Day parade down Archer Avenue ending up at the corner of Tripp where a World War II Memorial stood. I also remember that special time when we got the chance to go to the Cubs-Sox exhibition game that was played each summer. My best friend, Ron Kozinski – a die-hard Cub fan – (boy, did we have lots of discussions about who was the better Chicago team!) who also played Little League, and I went to the game at Comiskey Park. Our parents bought us tickets and we rode a school bus with the team and coaches to Comiskey on an over-cast weekday night. As a group from the West Lawn Little League we all sat together down the left field line close to the foul pole. It started drizzling a bit as the game started and although it really never let up; it didn't dampen the spirits of all the Little League ballplayers in the stands. As the game moved from inning to inning, the rain seemed to move from drizzle to steady rain.

Around the fifth inning, I suggested to my baseball buddy, Ron, that we go for a little walk around our seating area. We did and eventually we ventured further and further away from our West Lawn Little Leaguers and coaches. Eventually, we found ourselves behind the scoreboard. With the rain continuing and the score tied 6 – 6, the public address announcer came on to say, "Baseball fans, due to a concern for the baseball player's safety, tonight's Chicago Cubs and Chicago White Sox game has been called because of rain. We appreciated your attendance and please enjoy the fireworks show."

Almost immediately, the lights went out and the scoreboard fireworks began. Boom! Crack! Sizzle! Boom! How were we ever going to get back to our seats in the dark before our group headed for the busses? The aisles were filled with all sorts of kids in all sorts of different uniforms and caps. Chaperones were calling out to their kids to stick together and head for the exits. Ron and I knew we would be in big trouble if we didn't get back to our group because there were dozens and dozens of school busses outside and we knew we would never find ours.

Miraculously – to this day I still don't know how we did it – we managed to hook up with our fellow West Lawn Little Leaguers and headed for our busses. Needless to say, we never told our parents about our adventure, but this night still stands out in my memory as one of my all-time favorites. I lost track of Ron after high school, but I'm sure he remembers this game as I do. Scary! Funny! Cool! We were growing up.

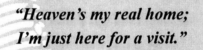

*"Heaven's my real home;
I'm just here for a visit."*

—Lorn Brown

The popular and affable Brown served two different stints as an analyst for White Sox broadcasts from 1976-1979 and 1983-1988. He also announced games for the Milwaukee Brewers and New York Mets, where he was affectionately known as "The Professor" because of his greying hair and glasses, plus wearing a vest and tweed jacket while on the air.

Chapter 5

The Rise and Fall of the Chicago White Sox

The 2017 baseball season marks the 100th anniversary of the 1917 American League pennant winner and World Series championship of the Chicago White Sox. During those ten decades, Sox fans have endured some very difficult seasons . . . way too many!

For some fans, baseball is not just a sport, but a generational experience. In my case, being born and raised in Chicago allowed me to experience and appreciate baseball through my dad and my two older brothers. Even my mother enjoyed going to a game once in awhile. When I was five years old, my family moved from the North Side where my parents tried – unsuccessfully – to run a small mom and pop neighborhood grocery store near the old Riverview Amusement Park. After six months they realized that it was best to sell the place, which they did, and moved our family to southwest Chicago, near Archer and Harlem. When I was about ten-years old, my parents decided that they had enough money to buy a three flat building. We moved to 48th and Keeler Avenue. It was closer to where my dad worked his whole life – Crane Company located in Brighton Park. It also happened to get us a little closer to Comiskey Park!

After the 1917 World Series, the White Sox struggled the following season. Several of their players spent time in the military as the United States entered the First World War. The 1918 abbreviated campaign (124 games) was a dismal one record-wise as the Sox fell to 57-67. Following his banner 1917 year, ace Eddie Cicotte led the league in losses with 19. The Sox were just flat in 1918 finishing seventeen games behind the American League champion Boston Red Sox. The White Sox were mired in sixth place as the season ended.

1919 would be different to say the least. Besides rebounding with an 88-52 record, the team finished in first place 3½ games ahead of the second place Cleveland Indians. The Sox were poised to win their second World Series championship in three years and third since 1906. They were the heavy favorites to defeat the Cincinnati Reds. However, the influence of gamblers who wanted to cash in on a heavy favorite losing to the underdog, caused eight of the White Sox players to conspire to throw the 1919 World Series. There has been a lot written about whether all of the eight players were in on the fix, but the result was the same: The White Sox lost to Cincinnati five games to three in a series that was enlarged to a best-of-nine in order to raise money for war veterans. The players implicated were: "Shoeless" Joe Jackson, Happy Felsch, Buck Weaver, Swede Risberg, Fred McMullin, Chick Gandil, "Lefty" Williams, and Eddie Cicotte.

Of the eight players who would be banned with only a few games remaining in the 1920 season, five were solid players who could have formed the nucleus of some great ball clubs had they stayed clean. These players were Jackson, Felsch, Weaver, Williams, and Cicotte. Evidence of this was that even though the Sox lost the 1919 World Series, the team came right back and were in the thick of the 1920 pennant race. Entering the final week of the season, the Sox found themselves one half game behind the American League-leading Cleveland Indians. The Sox season would be decided, not on the baseball diamond, but in a Chicago courtroom. The verdict on whether the eight players who had been indicted for throwing the 1919 World Series was . . . not guilty! The reason was that the confessions of the players had been lost and the jury used this as the reason to acquit the players. Baseball Commissioner, Judge Kennesaw Mountain Landis felt differently. The day after the players' acquittal, Landis handed down his ruling: "Regardless of the verdict of juries, no player that throws a ballgame; no player that undertakes or promises to throw a ballgame; no player that sits in a conference with a bunch of crooked players and gamblers where the ways and means of throwing games are planned and discussed and does not promptly tell his club about it, will ever play professional baseball."

The 1920 season ended with the Sox two games behind the American League pennant winner Cleveland Indians. Thereafter, the Sox would see the first division in the American League only six times during the next thirty years. The team never finished higher than third during this period. It wouldn't be until the Go-Go Sox of the 1950s that the White Sox would be true contenders once again. From 1952 through 1956, the Sox finished third each season. In 1957 and 1958 they finished second. In 1959, the White Sox won the American League pennant. The decision by the eight Black Sox players in 1919 had a devastating effect on the history of the franchise. A once budding dynasty came to a screeching halt with the banishment of five of its most productive players. The result was a team that struggled for more than three decades. Yet, loyal Chicago White Sox fans remained faithful. They could only dream of what might have been?

"I would always sing it

(Take Me Out To The Ballgame)

because I think it's the only

song I knew the words to."

—Harry Caray

White Sox play-by-play radio announcer from 1971-1981. Caray first sang, *Take Me Out To The Ballgame,* during the seventh inning stretch while broadcasting White Sox games. It became a tradition when he moved to the North Side to broadcast Chicago Cubs games in 1982. Caray's broadcasting career included stints with the St. Louis Browns, Oakland Athletics, and St. Louis Cardinals before working for the White Sox and Cubs. In 1989, Caray was admitted into the National Baseball Hall of Fame upon receiving the Ford C. Frick Award for broadcasting.

5th Inning

THE SOX IN THE SEVENTIES - THE BIG RED MACHINE

I was in college attending Northern Illinois University on my way to become a life-long educator when the Sox experienced a fun resurgence in the 1970's. The South Side Hitmen came on the scene with a cast of power hitters that hadn't been seen before. Picking up on Cincinnati's "Big Red Machine" theme led by Hall of Famers Johnny Bench and Joe Morgan, and wannabe HOF'er Pete Rose, that saw the Reds win two World Series in 1970 and '71, the White Sox had their version. Sporting red on white uniforms, the Sox had an explosive team led by Greg "The Bull" Luzinski and "Beltin" Bill Melton.

This team was amazing in setting off the centerfield scoreboard hundreds of times in the '70s. This was a fun bunch that generated lots of interest because the Sox team was being transformed from a relatively weak hitting team to one that relied on the homeroom to produce wins.

I followed the Sox closely, attending games whenever I could. I remember one night game when my cousin, Shirley, and her husband, Bill, went to a game with Ann and me. We sat behind third base and talked Sox baseball all night. Shirley and Bill are great

Sox fans and have followed them all of their lives. Shirley graduated from Queen of Peace High School in Burbank, while Bill was a transfer from St. Ignatius to St. Laurence High School that is right next door to Queen of Peace. I didn't know Bill while I was at Laurence, even though we graduated together in 1968. Shirley was one of my cousins who were all about the same age. Growing up in Chicago we had many fun times together. We enjoyed each other's company at frequent family get-togethers – weddings, anniversaries, birthdays, and unfortunately some sad times, too, like funerals. But, we were all family and Shirley was not only a fun person, but also an avid Sox fan.

I don't know who won the game we attended together, but we had a memorable time . . . at least for me! We ate hot dogs and downed a beer or two while sitting in our seats and watching the game unfold on the field. Unable to finish some food that I had ordered from a friendly vendor, I remember Shirley saying to me, "Mark, your eyes are bigger than your stomach!" I still remember that. I wonder if Shirley does?

One of the players Shirley and Bill really liked was Eric Soderholm, a good hitting right-handed batter who played a solid third base. Maybe they liked him for another reason? Their son is named, Eric!

The South Side Hitmen energized Chicago and made fans believe that they could win it all. What a line-up that took the field for Opening Day in 1977 versus the Toronto Blue Jays:

Ralph Garr, *Leftfield*

Alan Bannister, *Shortstop*

Jorge Orta, *Second base*

Richie Zisk, *Rightfield*

Jim Spencer, *First base*

Oscar Gamble, *Designated hitter*

Eric Soderholm, *Third base*

Chet Lemon, *Centerfield*

Brian Downing, *Catcher*

Ken Brett, *Pitcher*

The Sox were in the pennant chase throughout much of the season, jumping into first place in the American League West Division ahead of the Minnesota Twins and Kansas City Royals on July 1st. They stayed there until August 12th when they began their fade into third place, twelve games behind the Royals. The Sox won 90 games, but Kansas City had an even more tremendous one winning 102. The Sox hit a record-setting team record of 192 home runs that year. The South Side Hitmen were a big hit for Sox fans!

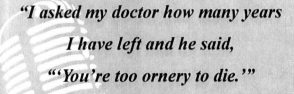

"I asked my doctor how many years
I have left and he said,
"'You're too ornery to die.'"

—Jimmy Piersall

Following a seventeen-year playing career with the Boston Red Sox, Cleveland Indians, Washington Senators, New York Mets, Los Angeles Angels, and California Angels, Piersall teamed with Harry Caray to broadcast White Sox games from 1977-1981.

Chapter Six

Great Games in White Sox History

As mentioned earlier, the 2017 baseball season marks one hundred years of baseball being played by the Chicago White Sox since their 1917 World Series Championship. During that time, the White Sox have played nearly 16,000 baseball games. In addition, since their entrance into the American League in 1901, the White Sox have played in almost 18,000 games. Remember that the regular season consisted of 154 games until 1961 when, due to expansion, the season was extended to what it is today: 162 games. The Major League Baseball strike in the mid-nineties caused a huge disruption, as well as an interruption of games played. Labor disputes between the players and owners resulted in the 1994 season being canceled after 113 games. The dispute did not end until April of 1995. The regular season was shortened to 144 games that year. Through it all, nearly 18,000 games, have been played in Comiskey Park, or the "new" Comiskey — U.S. Cellular Field — now named Guaranteed Rate Field.

Looking back at all of the games the White Sox have played in their franchise history, how does one pick games of note? When writing this book, I thought about the many seasons I have followed

– nearly 50! Yet, there are at least another 50 seasons that were played from 1917-2017 that I have only had the opportunity to read or, in some cases, hear stories about from people who talked about their own experiences at the ballpark.

I invite readers to do their own research to find out more information about the many seasons of the White Sox. What I did was look back at the past 100 years of White Sox baseball and select a special or unique game from each of the ten decades that the White Sox have played over the past one hundred years. That makes ten games that standout in my mind. It could have been dozens – or possibly hundreds. But, selecting ten games gets the point across: baseball is a great game and has many intriguing nuances. Just as hitters dig in at the plate, I ask readers to step up to the plate to provide their own best memories.

Great Game Number 1
Decade: 1917 – 1927
Game Six of the 1917 World Series
Monday, October 17, 1917
Polo Grounds, New York
"The Clincher!"

I've already explained how the White Sox triumphantly ended their record-setting season and their subsequent victory over the New York Giants to claim the 1917 World Series. Game Six of the Series, the final game, was one for the ages for White Sox fans. Here's why.

Two errors in the fourth inning by the Giants – one on a ground ball hit by Eddie Collins to shortstop Heinie Zimmerman who threw wildly to first and a second error when Giants' rightfielder Dave Robertson dropped a fly ball hit by Joe Jackson – resulted in

Chicago runners at the corners with Happy Felsch coming to the plate with no outs having been recorded. The scoreless game was going to change and change dramatically in favor of the White Sox.

Felsch hit a routine grounder back to Giant starting pitcher Rube Benton. What should have been a simple play turned out to be the game changer.

Collins, at third, broke for the plate and Benton threw to Giant third baseman Zimmerman who ran Collins down towards the plate. Collins somehow maneuvered himself around catcher Bill Rariden and now it was a foot race between Collins and Zimmerman to home. No one for New York had bothered to protect the plate! Speedy Eddie Collins won the foot race giving the White Sox a 1-0 lead. As the runners – Jackson and Felsch – moved up to second and third, Chick Gandil then stroked a two-run single tallying two more runs. The Sox held on for a 4-2 victory as "Red" Faber won his third game of the Series. Faber was one of the obvious heroes of the Series having pitched two complete game victories (Games 2 and 6), as well as winning one in relief (Game 5). Can you imagine coming back to start what became the final game of the World Series after only two days' rest – going all nine innings? Yes, "Red" Faber was one of the heroes of the 1917 World Series.

Eddie Collins batted .409 in the Series, while Buck Weaver contributed with a .333 average. Joe Jackson batted .304 to bolster an offense that kept the Giants off center for four of the six games of the World Series; enough to capture baseball's championship.

Great Game Number 2
Decade: 1927 – 1937
Thursday, July 6, 1933
Comiskey Park, Chicago, Illinois
The First All-Star Game

Historic Comiskey Park was the site for the very first Major League All-Star Game played in July, 1933. In attendance were nearly 49,000 fans to see the greatest ballplayers at the time take the field. Why Chicago?

The Great Depression had taken its toll on baseball attendance as it dropped 40% in the early 1930s. What would help increase fan interest in America's pastime?

Interestingly, the 1933 World's Fair was being held in Chicago. The newspaper owner of the *Chicago Tribune*, Colonel Robert McCormick, and his sports editor, Arch Ward, suggested that baseball hold a one-time extravaganza that would have the greatest stars of the game showcase their talents. The aim was to bring interested fans through the turnstiles. What better city to host this historic game then in Chicago – at legendary Comiskey Park?

Fans were encouraged to vote for their favorite players and voting took place in fifty-five newspapers around the United States. Hundreds of thousands of fans participated in the balloting. Elected to the American League and National League rosters was a cross-section of baseball's elite. The two leagues featured the following starting line-ups:

National League (Manager: John McGraw)

3B	Pepper Martin	(St. Louis Cardinals)
2B	Frankie Frisch	(St. Louis Cardinals)
RF	Chuck Klein	(Philadelphia Phillies)
LF	Chick Hafey	(Cincinnati Reds)
1B	Bill Terry	(New York Giants)
CF	Wally Berger	(Boston Braves)
SS	Dick Bartell	(Philadelphia Phillies)
C	Jimmie Wilson	(St. Louis Cardinals)
P	Bill Hallahan	(St. Louis Cardinals)

American League (Manager: Connie Mack)

LF	Ben Chapman	(New York Yankees)
2B	Charlie Gehringer	(Detroit Tigers)
RF	Babe Ruth	(New York Yankees)
1B	Lou Gehrig	(New York Yankees)
CF	Al Simmons	(Chicago White Sox)
3B	Jimmy Dykes	(Chicago White Sox)
SS	Joe Cronin	(Washington Senators)
C	Rick Ferrell	(Boston Red Sox)
P	"Lefty" Gomez	(New York Yankees)

Twenty of the thirty-six players selected to participate in the first All-Star Game would become Hall of Famers. Two White Sox players who gained Cooperstown fame were Simmons and Dykes. Interestingly, selected as a reserve for the National League team was Tony Cuccinello, a second baseman for the Brooklyn Dodgers. I mention Cuccinello because old number 33 was the third base coach for the Chicago White Sox when they won the American League pennant in 1959. Besides "Cooch," serving as reserves on the benches for both the AL and NL All-Stars were future Hall of Famers Gabby Hartnett, Carl Hubbell, Pie Traynor, Paul Waner (all members of the senior circuit National League team) and Bill Dickey, Jimmy Foxx, "Lefty" Grove, and Tony Lazzeri (for the American League). What a star-studded lineup! What a special night for baseball fans, especially in Chicago!

The American League emerged victorious in this All-Star studded classic, 4-2. Babe Ruth hit a two-run homer in the bottom of the third inning and made a great catch in the top of the eighth when he went up against the right field scoreboard to haul in a long fly. The winning pitcher was "Lefty" Gomez.

The All-Star Game would become a fixture in baseball for seasons to come. The Midsummer Classic had captured the imagination of baseball fans . . . and it all started right in Chicago at "The Palace" – Comiskey Park!

Great Game Number 3
Decade: 1937 – 1947
April 28, 1946
Comiskey Park, Chicago, Illinois
Hall of Famer Ted Lyons Final Game

One hour and 41 minutes. That's how long it took for Ted Lyons to win his 260th game. Then, it was over. A career that spanned 21 Major League seasons – all with the White Sox – came to an end on Sunday April 28, 1946 at Comiskey Park. Why is this game and career so important?

Lyons toiled for teams that were not very good. Yet, "Sunday Teddy" amassed the most wins in White Sox franchise history.

Lyons never pitched a game in the minors.

Lyons career record was 260-230 including 356 complete games. He recorded 1,073 strikeouts and had a career earned run average of 3.67. During his 21 campaigns, the White Sox finished fifth or lower in the eight team American League sixteen times. The highest the Sox finished during his tenure on the team was third place. He won 20 games three times and during his pitching career led the American League in victories twice. His best season was in 1930 when he went 22-15 hurling for a ball club that finished in sixth place, 40 games behind the first place Philadelphia Athletics. Lyons won 22 of the Sox 62 victories as the Sox went 62-92 overall.

Lyons was such a fan favorite that near the end of his career, White Sox Manager Jimmy Dykes decided to exclusively pitch him on Sunday afternoon games.

How good was Ted Lyons? Hall of Fame Yankee Manager Joe McCarthy once said that, "If he had pitched for the Yankees, he would have won over 400 games."

Lyons beat the St. Louis Browns on the front end of a Sunday doubleheader that April Sunday afternoon, 4-3. It was his 28th straight complete game! Ted Lyons was inducted into the Hall of Fame in 1955. The White Sox retired his number 16 in 1987.

I never saw Lyons pitch, but I wish I had!

Oh, by the way, Lyons won his first two games of his career in 1923 in unique fashion. Summoned to relieve in both ends of a doubleheader against the Browns in St. Louis, Lyons won both contests! He was really something!

Great Game Number 4
Decade: 1947 – 1957
Tuesday, May 1, 1951
Comiskey Park, Chicago, Illinois
Minnie Minoso's White Sox Debut

The 1950s were an exciting time for the White Sox. There was a sense that something special was beginning to take shape on the South Side. For example, 1951 brought a new form of excitement to fans who came to the ballpark in record numbers as the White Sox drew one million fans for the first time in their history. The "Go-Go" White Sox were on their way to end their drought.

On May 1, 1951, the White Sox chose Orestes "Minnie" Minoso to be their first black player. In his very first plate appearance, Minoso hit a home run against Yankee righthander Vic Raschi. The 14,776 fans in attendance that Tuesday evening were not only treated to Minoso's debut, but also a glimpse of what was about to happen in the years that followed. Minnie got two hits in his four plate appearances, had two RBI, and scored a run. Playing third base, Minoso also started a double play. The Sox ended up losing to the Yankees 8-3, but a new era had begun on the South Side.

Minoso went on to a very successful career that many would say, myself included, was Hall of Fame worthy. The "Cuban Comet" played seventeen years in the Big Leagues for four different teams. Minnie actually had five different stints with the White Sox (1951-1957, 1960-1961, 1964, 1976, and 1980). Minoso broke into the majors in 1949 with the Cleveland Indians, so when he batted as a White Sox in 1980, he became the only player ever to play in five decades! He was 55 years old and still in great shape, something that Minoso always maintained throughout his life.

Minoso collected 1,963 hits over his career that included 186 home runs, 1,023 RBIs, and 205 stolen bases. His career batting average was .298. In his rookie year, Minoso batted .324, but did not earn Rookie of the Year honors. That distinction went to Yankee Gil McDougal who batted .306. Minoso had 622 plate appearances, while McDougal had 473. Statistically, Minoso had a better year, but the baseball writers voted in favor of McDougal as the American League Rookie of the Year.

Why has Minnie not been inducted into the Hall? One reason may be due to the color barrier that existed in baseball when Minoso first started playing. Minoso played his first three years in the Cuban Negro League and then two years for the Cleveland Indians minor league club. Plus, his career numbers tailed off after an injury with the St. Louis Cardinals in 1962.

However, the value that Minnie Minoso brought to the Chicago White Sox, and even more important, to the game of baseball itself, was his endearing love of the game and in return the love of fans for him. He is one of the greatest players in White Sox history. His successful debut on May 1, 1951 set into motion a truly wonderful relationship between baseball fans everywhere and the great number 9, Orestes "Minnie" Minoso!

Great Game Number 5
Decade: 1957 – 1967
Wednesday, April 22, 1959
Municipal Stadium, Kansas City, Missouri
White Sox Score 11 Runs in One Inning . . . on One Hit!

There was a sense in Chicago that the 1959 season was going to be very special for White Sox fans. The "Go-Go" White Sox had played consistent ball throughout the 1950s. For example, although the '51 ball club finished in fourth place, they were playing exciting baseball. The 1952 season began a string of five consecutive third place finishes. The 1957 and 1958 seasons saw the White Sox finish in second place to the New York Yankees. Fans saw the opportunity that a pennant was possible in 1959.

1959 was also the first year I really began understanding the game of baseball. I had watched my first World Series between the Milwaukee Braves and New York Yankees the previous two Octobers, and although I grasped the importance of the Fall Classic, it wasn't until the 1959 season that I really was getting into White Sox baseball. I guess being nine years old was the difference!

I remember listening to a 1959 White Sox game on radio as they played a road game against the Kansas City Athletics. Little did I know that this early season game was going to be one of the strangest – and memorable – games in White Sox history!

I know for most Sox fans, 1959 is a long way back in the past. But, it's games like the one played on April 22, 1959 that gets stuck in your memory. It's been a long time for me, too. In fact, so long that although I remember listening to the game, I had to Google information so I could recreate this extremely unusual game in my mind and for you. Here's what happened in old Municipal Stadium in Kansas City on a late April night in the White Sox pennant winning season. It was a doozey . . . and one for the record books.

First off, I bet if you asked an old K.C. Athletics fan if they remembered this game, you would probably get a 100,000 people to say they not only remember it, they were there! But, in fact, there were only 7,446 on hand to witness a baseball oddity that still stands today.

The Sox won the game, 20-6. That would seem like a major feat for a team that was not big on scoring runs or getting lots of hits. This night was different. They scored plenty of runs, especially in one inning, but still on only one hit!

For the record, the 1959 White Sox ranked sixth in offense in the eight team American League. The team batting average for the season was .250 with 620 total RBIs and were last hitting home runs with 97 for the entire year!

In the seventh inning, the White Sox were winning 8-6. Their ace, Early Wynn, had been chased earlier in the game as the Athletics scored five runs in the second inning to take a 6-1 lead. But, the Sox came back in dramatic and somewhat humorous fashion at the expense of some frustrated pitchers and hapless fielders. How can you score eleven runs in one inning on only one hit? First of all, you do it by coaxing the most bases loaded walks in a game that remains a Major League Baseball record.

First baseman Ray Boone started the "walk" parade by actually reaching first on an error by the Kansas City shortstop Joe DeMaestri. Al Smith followed by also reaching first via an error by third baseman Hal Smith as he tried to bunt Boone to second. Right fielder Johnny Callison singled to right scoring both Boone and Smith due to an error by K.C. right fielder Roger Maris. Callison went all the

74

way to third on the play. Next up was future Hall of Famer Louie Aparicio who coaxed a walk and promptly stole second base. Pitcher Bob Shaw strolled to the plate and continued onto first as he was given a base on balls. Earl Torgeson pinch hit for Sammy Esposito and walked allowing Callison to score. The great Nellie Fox came to the plate and was given his own free pass to first as teammate Aparicio crossed the plate. Fleet-footed center fielder Jim Landis hit a ground ball to the pitcher who threw to the catcher for a force and the first out of the inning. Catcher Sherm Lollar came to the batter's box and received a free pass to first scoring Torgeson. Ray Boone batted for the second time in the inning and received his own walk scoring Fox. Al Smith came up-to-bat for his second time and received a base on balls scoring Landis. Next up was Callison who was promptly hit by a pitch that plated Lollar. Lou Skizas entered the game as a pinch runner for Callison. Little Louie came up next and received his second walk of the inning, Boone scoring. Bubba Phillips pinch hit for Torgeson and walked scoring Al Smith. Nellie Fox then received his second walk of the inning allowing pinch runner Skizas to score. Landis ended the Athletics misery by grounding out, pitcher to first. It took three Kansas City pitchers to finally retire the side. Tom Gorman started the fateful seventh inning, but didn't get anyone out and yet was charged with six runs – only two earned – and the lone hit of the inning. He also issued three walks. Mark Freeman entered the game and was touched for two unearned runs while also issuing two walks of his own. George Brunet was summoned to put down the White Sox uprising, which he did but not before walking five batters and giving up three runs.

What a game! Believe me, it was something to listen to on the radio that late April evening. I bet many old-time White Sox fans remember that night, too!

Great Game Number 6
Decade: 1967 – 1977
1977 Season: "South Side Hitmen!"
Friday, Saturday, and Sunday, July 1-3, 1977
Minnesota Twins vs. Chicago White Sox
Comiskey Park, Chicago, Illinois

The 1977 season was a remarkable one for the White Sox. Although they finished in third place and a distant twelve games behind the West Division winning Kansas City Royals and second place Texas Rangers, the White Sox had a very successful season winning ninety games while losing seventy-two. Chicago fans were treated to an exciting team that won forty-eight games at home while dropping thirty-three. However, the first half of the season was exciting for all Chicago baseball fans as both the Cubs and White Sox were in first place at the All-Star break – the first time that had happened since 1906. Also, White Sox fans saw a powerful team that established a then single season-high franchise record for home runs hitting 192 dingers. That record stood until 1996 when that club hit 195 homers. In all, the White Sox had nine players who banged out ten or more home runs on the season. Leading the way was Oscar Gamble (31), followed by Richie Zisk (30), Eric Soderholm (25), Chet Lemon (19), Lamar Johnson (18), Jim Spencer (18), Jorge Orta (11), Jim Essian (10), and Ralph Garr (10). Hence, the team became known as the "South Side Hitmen." White Sox announcers Harry Caray, Jimmy Piersall, Lorn Brown, and Mary Shane on WMAQ radio provided a steady diet of excitement and enthusiasm to fans listening closely at home, in the yard or garage, or wherever they might be to find time to catch a game. There was excitement everywhere in Chicago!

Midway through the 1977 season, the Minnesota Twins visited

Chicago for a four game series starting with a Friday night and Saturday afternoon contests. The four game set culminated with a Sunday doubleheader. The White Sox started the series eight games over .500 with a 40-32 record. After sweeping the Twins by scores of 5-2, 13-8, 6-0, and 10-8, the White Sox record stood at 44-32 and in first place atop the American League West Division. Friday night's weather was hot – 85 degrees at game time – and was played before 35,709 fans who saw the White Sox play a sturdy defense in capturing the first game of the series. At bat, Richie Zisk paced Chicago by hitting two home runs, his 19th and 20th of the year. The White Sox rallied in Saturday's game scoring seven runs in the bottom of the eighth inning to go onto the 13-8 victory. Strangely, no White Sox hit a home run much to the disappointment of the 26,957 fans in attendance. Sunday's first game had southpaw Wilbur Wood even his record at 2-2 while going the distance in a 6-0 victory. He didn't need homers that day as he once again dazzled batters with his knuckleball. Wood was no stranger of going the distance as he completed 114 games of the 297 games he started during his seventeen-year Major League career. The nightcap of the doubleheader saw the White Sox club three home runs. Jim Spencer, Jim Essian, and Alan Bannister all hit roundtrippers in the 10-8 win.

Why consider this series of games between the Twins and White Sox being significant in the 1967-1977 decade? I could have selected other events and games like the White Sox traveling to Milwaukee to play games to help boost attendance during the 1968-69 season. The Brew City had lost its Braves team to Atlanta in 1966. In 1969, AstroTurf was installed in the infield of "The Palace." "Beltin' Bill" Melton set the all-time White Sox record for home runs in 1971. The White Sox wore shorts instead of pants three times during the 1976 season. All could have made for interesting stories, but the 1977 season and the July 1-3 series versus Minnesota typified that the White Sox were becoming: Home Run Hitters. The "South Side Hitmen" electrified fans during the 1977 season and a sweep of any team at home while occupying first place deserves recognition.

Great Game Number 7
Decade: 1977 – 1987
Thursday, July 12, 1979
Detroit Tigers vs. Chicago White Sox
Comiskey Park, Chicago, Illinois
Disco Demolition Night!

Twi-night doubleheaders. What fun! What a bargain, right? Hey, how about adding a promotion promising to explode thousands of disco records in-between games of the doubleheader? Leave it to master promoter and White Sox owner Bill Veeck to plan an event like this. What Veeck didn't plan for was a near riot and the forfeiture of the nightcap of the twin-bill.

The 1970s saw the rise in popularity of disco. Songs, movies, and dances were all around and although many people loved the genre, others loathed it. Veeck came up with the idea to capitalize on the latter and in the process hoped to get some additional fans through the turnstiles. He got more than he bargained for.

What's lost in this event is where did the White Sox stand won/loss-wise during the 1979 season? Well, it would be fun to say that Chicago was in the pennant race, but that wasn't to be. On the morning of July 12, 1979 – getting ready to play games 87 and 88 of the season – the White Sox found themselves in fifth place with a record of 40-46 in the American League West Division. They remained mired in fifth place as the season ended finishing with a 73-87 record. Disappointing, yes. And that's one of the reasons why Bill Veeck planned a special night to draw fans...and to destroy disco.

Popular Chicago radio disc jockey Steve Dahl was invited to be the master of ceremonies in-between games one and two of the doubleheader. Dahl's job was to hype the event on his radio show and then rally the troops at the game. No one knew exactly what the response would be to the promotion. Remember, the White Sox were having a sub-par season. Would 10,000 people attend? 20,000? What would you say if the crowd approached 50,000 people? That's right; 50,000 fans attended the game that charged 98 cent admission and a vinyl record that would be blown up in-between games. The crowd was raucous in anticipation of the between game festivities. Some fans even tossed vinyl records like Frisbees around Comiskey Park. Woodstock it wasn't, but the fans in the stands were having the time of their lives.

The White Sox lost the first game as the Tigers beat Chicago 4-1. Present day White Sox broadcaster, Ed Farmer, pitched shutout ball for the final 3 2/3 innings. The twenty minute intermission began with Steve Dahl coming onto the field dressed in military gear and wearing an Army helmet. The fans went wild in anticipation of something big about to happen. They weren't disappointed.

The mound of disco records that had been collected as fans passed through the turnstiles were placed in a big box in centerfield. There were fireworks leading up to the box and on command – the actual fireworks really didn't ignite on cue – the fireworks and box were set off. A large plume of smoke rose from the rubble and the crowd went wild and increasingly out-of-control. Remember, there was still a second game to be played and some of the players took the field – at their own risk – to begin warming up. Fans who had gained access to the field were asked on several occasions to remove themselves so the second game could proceed as planned. It wasn't to be. It became increasingly clear that the field had become unplayable in some areas and the umpires had no choice but to forfeit the second game of the doubleheader to the Tigers. Veeck was a showman, but on this night he'd gone too far.

Yet, it is a game – or at least an event – for the ages! No review of the history of the White Sox can leave Disco Demolition Night off one's list.

Great Game Number 8
Decade: 1987 – 1997
Thursday, July 1, 1990
New York Yankees vs. Chicago White Sox
Comiskey Park, Chicago, Illinois
Sox No-Hit – WIN!

The late 1980s and 1990s brought lots of excitement to the South Side. Plans for the "new" Comiskey Park were being set into motion keeping the White Sox in Chicago. Future Hall of Famer, Carlton "Pudge" Fisk cracked his 2,000 hit in 1989, and in 1990 set the home run record for catchers belting his 328th roundtripper. Later in 1993, Fisk caught his 2,226 game behind the plate breaking Bob Boone's career record. The date was Tuesday, June 23rd. I know because I was there! Also, 1990 saw the curtain coming down on old Comiskey Park with a White Sox victory over the Seattle Mariners, 2-1, on Sunday, September 30. The following season found Frank Thomas hitting his first home run in the first night game at the new Comiskey Park. Thomas would go onto a Hall of Fame career becoming the greatest offensive player in White Sox franchise history. The multi-talented Bo Jackson donned a White Sox uniform and helped the Pale Hose secure their second American League West title in 1993. Third baseman Robin Ventura hit two grand slams in one inning in 1985, equaling that same feat accomplished by eight previous players. And in 1997, the two Chicago teams met for the first time during the regular season as they competed in the Cross-Town Series. What an intra-city rivalry! Yes, there were many great moments during this decade. Yet, the game between the Yankees and the White Sox on the first day of July in 1990 is one for the ages.

Can a team win a game in which they are no-hit? In other words, can a team score enough runs without getting a single hit and still manage to win the game?

A Sunday afternoon crowd of 30,642 was on hand to see the last place Yankees (28-45, fifteen games behind the Oakland Athletics in the American League West Division) take on the second place White Sox (who were percentage points behind Oakland). The White Sox record stood at 46-26. It was a beautiful day at Comiskey Park as the temperature hovered around the mid-70s. Chicago at its finest!

Who knew that the bright sun and windy conditions coming off of Lake Michigan would play a role in this fascinating game?

Right-hander Andy Hawkins was on the mound for New York. Hawkins was not having a particular stellar year as his record stood at 1-4 with a 6.49 ERA. Yet, his performance that day made him look like Don Drysdale or Greg Maddux. The first batter for the White Sox, speedy centerfielder Lance Johnson, nearly reached first base on a single to left, but leftfielder Jim Leyritz made a sensational sliding catch on the short fly to left. Later in the game, rightfielder Sammy Sosa hit a ball that normally would have been a tape measure home run, but the wind blowing in over the left field stands knocked it down to a long fly out on the warning track. Both starting pitchers kept the opposing teams in check and the game was scoreless after 7½ innings. The White Sox hurler was left hander Greg Hibbard who was having his own fine game limiting the Yankees to only four hits in his seven innings of work until he was relieved by right-hander Barry Jones. Hawkins kept mowing down White Sox batters and he entered the 8th inning with his no-hitter intact. But, that's when the roof fell in on him. Two batters were retired on popups that became adventures for second baseman Steve Sax who fought off the wind and glare of the sun to make the catches. Then, Sammy Sosa hit a sharp grounder to Mike Blowers at third who let the ball play him and Sosa ended up at first with an error. The next two batters, Guillen and Johnson, walked to load the bases. Robin Ventura hit a fly to left that on any other day would have been routine and end the inning with no damage being done. But, Leyritz dropped the ball for an error allowing three White Sox runners to score the first runs of the game. Designated hitter Ivan Calderon lifted a fly ball that rightfielder Jesse Barfield completely lost in the sun. His error allowed Ventura to score the fourth run of the inning. Leftfielder Dan Pasqua ended the inning – and Hawkins' misery – by popping out to the shortstop for the third out. Hawkins walked off the field with his no-hitter still in hand, but on the short end of the 4-0 score. The Yankees got a runner aboard off lefthanded reliever Scott Radinsky. But any hopes for a Yankee rally died when the White Sox turned a 6-4-3 double play to end the game. The winning pitcher for Chicago was Jones who improve his record to 10-1 on the season. Hawkins took the defeat and to add injury to insult was not credited with a no-hitter since he only pitched eight innings.

The box score read:

Team	1	2	3	4	5	6	7	8	9		R	H	E
New York	0	0	0	0	0	0	0	0	0	-	0	4	3
Chicago	0	0	0	0	0	0	0	4	0	-	4	0	2

What a game!

Great Game Number 9
Decade: 1997 – 2007
Friday, October 7, 2005
Boston Red Sox vs. Chicago White Sox
Fenway Park, Boston, Massachusetts
"El Duque" to the Rescue!

The 2005 season was a magical one for the Chicago White Sox and its loyal fans. They had endured an 88-year drought from their last World Series in 1917. Yes, they had seen their Pale Hose win division titles, only to lose in the playoffs. Yes, they had cheered on their Go-Go White Sox to the World Series in 1959 only to see them defeated by the Los Angeles Dodgers. 2005 was different. It would not end with fans being disappointed. Quite the contrary; White Sox fans were ecstatic as they were treated to something very special during the playoffs and World Series.

Besides going wire to wire to win the American League Central Division with a 99-63 record (second in wins only to the 1917 World Champion White Sox), the way the Sox mowed down their opponents in the post season was remarkable. The White Sox went 11-1 in the playoffs and World Series. They swept the Boston Red Sox in the American League Division Series. They captured the American League Championship Series four games to one over the Los Angeles Angels. The march to greatness and baseball im-mortality continued as the White Sox swept the National League pennant winners, Houston Astros, to win their third World Series Championship. Fantastic run for a fantastic club!

It's hard to pick a single game from the 2005 playoffs – they were all exciting – or for the entire season for that matter, as the White Sox electrified the city with a brand of baseball not seen on the South Side in many a season.

A brief look at the regular season showed that the White Sox started from the gate in excellent fashion. Led by Manager Ozzie Guillen, they won their first two games and then after ten games, stood at 7-3. They never looked back. By the end of May, the White Sox were eighteen games over .500 at 35-17. At the end of June, the White Sox were 53-24. A few days later, they entered the All-Star break with a 57-29 record. The White Sox had a commanding nine game lead in the American League Central Division over second place Minnesota. What proved to be an even better situation for the White Sox was that the American League All-Stars defeated the National League All-Stars 7-5 in Comerica Park, home of the Detroit Tigers. The American League victory assured the American League pennant winners with home field advantage in the World Series. Following the All-Star break, the White Sox continued their charge to the division title by expanding their lead to 14½ games over second place Minnesota and Cleveland. Their record stood at 68-35 at the beginning of August. Yet, the team seemed to sputter from mid-August to the conclusion of the month, losing eight of nine including a seven game skid that cut their lead to seven games. August ended with the White Sox having an 80-51 record. September was a different story. The White Sox again surged with a seven game win streak to open the final month of the campaign. They polished off their fine season by winning eight of their last ten games. The magical regular season had come to a close with Chicago sporting a 99-63 record – second in season victories only to the 1917 Chicago White Sox. They won over the second place Cleveland Indians who found themselves six games back.

Now, onto the playoffs!

As division champions the White Sox first opponent was the Wild Card Red Sox. Although Boston finished the regular season with an identical 95-67 record with the Yankees, New York was awarded first place due to a tie-breaker with Boston as the Bronx Bombers won the season series between the two clubs. The Los Angeles Angels of Anaheim hosted the Yankees.

Why choose the third game of the opening playoff series versus the Red Sox as THE game of the 1997-2007 decade? First, it's not easy. Certainly there are so many games that fans could choose as their game of the decade. The 2005 season had so many such contests. And the 2005 playoffs? The White Sox had highlights galore while emerging victorious over Boston, Los Angeles, and then Houston in the World Series. Any White Sox fan would find it difficult to select one single game as THE game of that memorable series of games. Remember reliever Bobby Jencks being called in by Manager Ozzie Guillen in the 8th inning to stop the Astros: Guillen motioning to the bullpen that he wanted "The Big Boy?" Remember Paul Konerko's grand slam and Scott Podsednik's walk-off homer in Game 2? Or, how about the fact that Konerko hit a total of five homers in their playoff run? Or, A.J. Pierzynski's "steal" of first in Game 2 versus the Angels? Or, the fact that the starting pitchers during that memorable series were unstoppable? Or, how about the fourth and final game of the sweep of the Astros when the White Sox won, 1-0? So many exciting games in the season and post season. But, here's why I chose Game 3 of the opening playoff series versus all the rest. But, first let me frame the scene of the series against Boston.

The Red Sox were the reigning World Series Champions as they had finally ended their 86-year drought since their last World Championship in 1918. The Red Sox had another solid year winning 95 games while losing 67. They had every expectation that they would repeat as champions. Why not? The previous year they had won 98 games. The 2005 version was a solid team led by 2005 American League All-Stars Johnny Damon, David Ortiz, Manny Ramirez, and Jason Varitek, plus pitcher Matt Clement. The only thing standing in their way was a Chicago team that hadn't won a World Series in 88 years!

Games 1 and 2 in Chicago had gone the White Sox way as the home team won convincingly 14-2 in the first contest behind Jose Contreras, who had a 15-7 record during the regular season. Then, Mark Buehrle won the second game with relief help from Bobby Jencks, 5-4. At age 26, southpaw Buehrle had another strong regular season winning 16 and dropping 8. The White Sox had taken a commanding two game lead in the best-of-five game American League Division Series.

But, the White Sox were heading to Boston and they had to know the reigning World Series Champions were a team that would not relinquish their crown easily.

Game 3 was everything – and more – that a fan of baseball would want to experience, especially if one of the teams involved was your favorite. White Sox fans will always remember the drama of this game and that's why I chose Game 3 of the Red Sox – White Sox series as the greatest game of the decade.

Right-hander Freddy Garcia was the starter for the White Sox. He proved the right choice going five strong innings before being relieved in the sixth after giving up three earned runs, including a lead-off homer in the sixth by Manny Ramirez. Acquired by the White Sox the previous year from the Seattle Mariners, "The Chief" had a 14-8 record in 2005. Garcia joined Buehrle, Contreras, Jon Garland (18-10), and Orlando Hernandez (9-9) in a starting pitching corps that accounted for 72 of the 99 victories Chicago amassed in their 2005 championship season. Sox starters who took the mound in 2005 were amazing!

35,496 fans jammed Fenway Park on Friday, October 7, 2005 looking to enjoy a mid-afternoon contest in cloudy 75 degree temperatures. Little did fans know that this game would be one for the ages.

Boston fans knew that this could be the final game of a really good season, plus their chances to repeat as World Series champs. Win, and they continue to dig their way out of a two game deficit. Lose, and they go home for the winter. It was all on the line.

For White Sox fans, every series, every game, every inning, every pitch, meant ending their World Championship drought which now stood at 88 years. They also knew the Red Sox would not go down easily. They were the champs and they were playing in their shrine – Fenway Park. White Sox fans knew anything could happen if Game 3 did not go their way.

Garcia was holding onto a 4-2 lead as he entered the sixth inning. He was greeted by a long home run by Ramirez to cut the lead to 4-3. Manager Guillen decided that Garcia had run out of gas and called upon lefthander Damaso Marte to squash any hopes of a Boston rally. However, the opposite took place. Marte gave up a single and walks to load the bases with no outs. Guillen, once again went to the mound, this time to replace Marte with right-hander Orlando Hernandez.

Boston fans knew that with catcher Jason Varitek coming to the plate, Tony Graffanino on deck, and Johnny Damon in the hole, they had a great chance to not only tie the game, but also bust it wide open. If their hometown favorites did that and held on to win the game, Boston fans had hopes that this might change the entire complexion of the series. White Sox fans listening on the radio or glued to television sets also knew this was a pivotal moment, not only in the game, but the series. A series can hinge on a single moment and the moment of truth was upon the reliever being called in to put down the Red Sox rally.

Ozzie Guillen would turn out looking like a genius as he made the decision to have Hernandez try to pitch out of the jam of his life. Perhaps it was decisions like these that resulted in Guillen being named American League Manager of the Year. But, decisions like these either make or break a team. White Sox fans knew that their run in the playoffs – and their hopes for a World Series Championship – were resting on the shoulders and right arm of the 40 year-old veteran Hernandez, nicknamed "El Duque." A pitcher known for his high leg kick and an assortment of pitches, including the Euphus pitch – or very slow junk pitch.

Varitek dug in as he knew Hernandez would be pitching strikes. He knew that Hernandez had not been brought in to the game to merely pitch around him or get him to chase a bad pitch. Varitek knew that there was no place to put him and Hernandez wasn't going to throw pitches out of the strike zone for to do that might risk a walk forcing in the tying run. Varitek knew he would get a pitch to hit. He was ready. So, was Hernandez. The crafty veteran made Varitek chase his pitch and Varitek lofted an infield pop-up. One out. Next to the plate was Graffanino.

With one out, Boston's second baseman knew he was on the spot to get the runner on third in for their fourth and tying run. Any way he could, Graffanino was going to do his best to either get on or somehow get the runner from third in to score. Hernandez was determined, too. He knew what was on the line. Prevent Graffanino from getting on base or scoring that runner ninety feet away from the plate. Everyone was at the edge of their seats in Fenway and at home, or wherever fans were following the game. Graffanino worked the count to 3-2 and then proceeded to foul off three Hernandez pitches. On the next offering, Hernandez got the better of Graffanino as he popped up to the shortstop. Two outs. But, the Red Sox rally was still not over. Walking up to the plate was the fleet-footed all-star Johnny Damon. A righthand pitcher versus a lefthand batter. Who would have the advantage on this afternoon?

Damon worked the count to 3-2. Again, everything was on the

line. Tension could be felt throughout the ballpark. Damon fouled off "El Duque's" next delivery. Tension was heightened to an even greater degree.

This is precisely why Game 3 of the American League Division Series was selected as the game of the decade. Everything was on the line. A run scores and the game is tied. Two or more runs score and Boston takes the lead and perhaps the victory – and the momentum going into Game 4. Win Game 4 and the series returns to Chicago where who knows what will happen. Maybe the White Sox World Series drought will continue. Chicago's fine season would be for naught. Game 3 is THE game of the series. THE game of the White Sox playoff run. THE game of the 2005 season. THE game of the 1997-2007 decade. This game would define the White Sox drive for a World Series. And "El Duque" was the man of the hour.

On a 3-2 pitch – Damon tries to check his swing, but can't, and the umpire calls out strike three! Orlando Hernandez has retired the side after coming in with the bases loaded and no outs! The White Sox hold onto their 4-3 lead.

Hernandez pitches a scoreless seventh and eighth inning and then hands over the ball to Bobby Jencks who pitches a 1-2-3 ninth for the White Sox victory, 5-3. The Red Sox are history as their season comes to a close. The White Sox continue their run that eventually will make history!

What a game! A game for the ages! THE game of the decade!

Great Game Number 10
Decade: 2007 – 2017
Thursday, July 23, 2009
Tampa Bay Rays vs. Chicago White Sox
U.S. Cellular Field, Chicago, Illinois
PERFECTO! . . . and *"The Catch!"*

When you think of the word "perfect," what comes to mind?

For some people, perfect may mean the smile of da Vinci's Mona Lisa. For parents of a newborn, it may mean the first time they hold their precious one and feel the perfectness of their baby's skin or rub the soft little hairs on its head. A student scoring a 36 on their ACT test may qualify for being perfect. Or perhaps for religious people, perfect means the absence of sin. For a bowling enthusiast, perfect means rolling a 300 game, or a golfer hitting a hole in one. But in baseball, what is being perfect?

27 batters up. 27 batters down. No hits, No walks. No errors. Natta. Nothing. Only 27 men coming to the plate facing a pitcher who on that day or night has the magic going for him that denies a runner to reach first base. Perfection! A perfect game!

In the modern era of baseball starting in 1900 and up to the 23rd day of July, 2009, there had been fifteen perfect games pitched including Don Larsen's gem in the 1956 World Series. Little did the 28,036 fans who had tickets to the Tampa Bay Rays – White Sox afternoon game in late July, 2009 know they would be witnessing baseball history. Yes, Chicago won the game 5-0. But, it was the pitching performance by Mark Buehrle that will be remembered forever, especially in the minds of loyal White Sox fans. Oh yes, there's a catch late in the game, but . . . that's for later.

Mark Buehrle is one of those rare breed of pitchers that only comes around once in a lifetime. He was special in so many ways: reliable, great fielder, didn't waste time between tosses, great command of his pitches so as not to allow lots of walks, yet able to strike-out batters without having a great deal of velocity. He was a fine pitcher who eventually won 214 games while losing 160 games during his sixteen-year big league career. Buehrle spent twelve of those years with the White Sox compiling a 161-119 record. Number 56 was a five time All-Star, and a four-time Gold Glove Award winner.

He was also an instrumental force in the 2005 Chicago White Sox World Series Championship year. In a nutshell, Buehrle was the ace of the staff during much of his career with the White Sox. He also threw a no-hitter and on this sunny Chicago afternoon did something remarkable and very memorable, hurling a perfect game!

Reading a box score is interesting because it tells of the statistics that took place during the game. For example, how many hits did a player have, how many runs were scored, who was on the mound during the game, how many pitches were thrown, etc. But, the July 23, 2009 game's box score reveals something to the fan that is so unique and so simple that it is beauty in itself. The box score was:

Team	1	2	3	4	5	6	7	8	9	R	H	E
Rays	0	0	0	0	0	0	0	0	0	0	0	0
Sox	0	4	0	0	1	0	0	0	X	5	6	0

WP: Mark Buehrle (11-3)   **LP:** Scott Kazmir (4-6)
Home Runs: **TB:** None   **CWS:** Josh Fields (7)

Zeroes across the board for Tampa Bay. 27 batters up. 27 batters down. No hits, No walks. No errors. Natta. Nothing. In 2 hours and three minutes, Mark Buehrle had throttled the Rays striking out six and except for a few sharply hit balls to infielders and outfielders, was seemingly in complete control.

Then, came the ninth inning.

Players, fans, and broadcasters all knew what was transpiring on the field. The fans erupted after every out, especially after Buehrle completed five innings in perfect fashion. As out after out was recorded, White Sox fans cheered with great anticipation as to what they might experience if only perfection could continue through nine innings. The White Sox were in command after first baseman Josh Fields hit a grand slam deep into the left field stands in the second inning. Chicago tacked on another run in the fifth to make the score 5-0 and provide Buehrle with additional confidence as he mowed down batter after batter in Tampa Bay's lineup. He was perfect after eight innings. White Sox broadcaster Ken "Hawk" Harrelson exclaimed after the last out in the eighth inning – a line drive caught by Gordon Beckham at third: "Call your sons, call your daughters, call your family, call your friends. Mark Buehrle has a perfect game going into the ninth!"

Yes, the ninth inning and . . . *"The Catch!"*

Manager Ozzie Guillen made a defensive substitution that may have changed the complexion of the entire game. Guillen replaced leftfielder Carlos Quentin and moved Scott Podsednik from center field to his position. For defensive purposes, Dewayne Wise was inserted into the outfield in center.

Leading off the Rays' ninth was righthand hitter (in fact all three hitters in the ninth hit from the right side of the plate – a supposed advantage over a lefthanded pitcher like Buehrle) Gabe Kapler who worked Buehrle to a 2-2 count before hitting a long fly ball to deep left center field. It looked as if the perfect game was over as Wise ran furiously back, back towards the wall. At the last moment, as the entire ballpark became silent, Wise leapt to try to catch the ball and he appeared to do just that robbing Kapler of a home run. As Wise caught the ball, he hit the outfield fence jarring him forward to the ground with the ball now being juggled as he fell to the warning track. Somehow, Wise maintained his composure – and the ball – recording the first out of the ninth inning. It would have been a miraculous catch under any circumstance, but Wise's grab was so much more meaningful as it kept Buehrle's perfect game intact. Unbelievable! Harrelson announced, "Under the circumstances, one of the sensational catches I have ever seen in fifty years in this game!"

Fans attending Chicago home games can still see the exact spot where Dewayne Wise leapt and hit the wall to make the catch. In fact, that's exactly what it says on the wall: *"The Catch!"* What a grab by Wise and what a smart defensive move by Manager Guillen at the top of the ninth inning! But, still there were two more batters for Mark Buehrle to retire to gain baseball immortality.

The next batter, Rays' catcher Michel Hernandez worked the count to 3-2 before Buehrle struck him out swinging. The final batter between history and what might be classified as a might have been was shortstop Jason Bartlett. Buehrle fell behind two and one, before Bartlett rolled a grounder to Alexei Ramirez at short who scooped up the three hopper and delivered a clean throw to Fields at first to complete the ecstasy of a perfect game for Mark Buehrle. As you can well imagine, there was a release of emotion as the drama of a perfect game had drained everyone. Buehrle was mobbed by his teammates, and Dewayne Wise, the hero of the moment in the ninth inning was also congratulated by the players, but most of all by an appreciative Buehrle. History had been made! A perfecto! In my opinion, the game of the decade on the South Side of Chicago!

There you have it. Ten special games over a century of seasons played by the Chicago White Sox. Most certainly, there will be many who would say that there were others that should have been considered as just as meaningful and special. I have no qualms with someone disagreeing with my choices. There are so many possibilities. Where do you start? These ten games represent the essence of what the White Sox were all about over a century of playing ball on the South Side of the Windy City. I ask that you think of what games you would have included on your list of special games or moments by the Chicago White Sox? Hopefully, some of the games detailed here would be among them.

"It wasn't a 'rooftop' shot, but it was a long, long home run."

—Joe McConnell

McConnell broadcast for the White Sox from 1980-1984 … the Winning Ugly Years! During his long career, McConnell broadcast professional football twenty-three seasons for the Denver Broncos, Minnesota Vikings, Chicago Bears, Indianapolis Colts, and Tennessee Titans, as well as seven seasons in the National Basketball Association for the Phoenix Suns and Indiana Pacers. Besides the White Sox, McConnell announced games for the Minnesota Twins. For fifteen years, he was the football play-by-play announcer for the Purdue Boilermakers upon his retirement in 2009.

6th Inning

WINNING UGLY!

WHO CAN REMEMBER WHAT TEAM HOLDS

THE RECORD FOR WINNING THE DIVISION?

I can!

The 1983 White Sox team had a record of 99-73 and won the American League West championship by 20 games! The second place Kansas City Royals actually had a below .500 record at 79-83. No team before or after has had a larger margin between first and second place than the 1983 Chicago White Sox.

The Sox had a very memorable year. The team was special and Sox fans then, as they should now, remember the tremendous season of 1983.

Led by Manager Tony La Russa, the Sox had some very memorable team members, some of whom received special honors. For example: Winning the American League Rookie of the Year Award was Ron Kittle. Kittle set a club record for most home runs hit by a rookie missing the American League home run title by three home runs while finishing third overall in the league. Winning the

American League Cy Young Award was LaMarr Hoyt with a 24-10 record. Hoyt started 34 games and completed eleven. Teammate Floyd Bannister finished second in the American League in strike-outs. Plus, Banister won 13 of 14 games after the All-Star Break going 16-10 overall on the season. The opening day lineup for the White Sox featured:

- *Rudy Law, cf*
- *Tony Bernazard, 2b*
- *Harold Baines, rf*
- *Greg Luzinski, dh*
- *Greg Walker, 1b*
- *Tom Paciorek, lf*
- *Carlton Fisk, c*
- *Vance Law, 3b*
- *Scott Fletcher, ss*
- *LaMarr Hoyt, p*

Texas Rangers manager, Doug Rader, gave the 1983 Sox team a special nickname. Rader said, "The Sox were not just playing well, they were playing ugly." It stuck. The '83 Sox team won so many games in different ways that they were just winning "ugly."

The following season was ugly, too, but for a different reason. Picked to win the American League West again, the Sox finished in 5th place with a 74-88 record. Although Sox fans' hopes were dashed, there was a feeling that the team was on the right track and the dream of an American League pennant winner and

World Series Championship would soon follow. Sox fans would have to be patient. It wouldn't be until the 1990's and the acquisition of Frank Thomas that Sox fans would become true believers. And it would take 20 plus years for the record-setting White Sox of 1983 to reach the mountaintop – winning the World Series in 2005. But, it was worth their patience. As the saying goes, "Good things happen to those who wait!"

"A nice 4-6-3, Hawkeroo."

"It looked like the wind held that one up. Lance Johnson got on his horse and man, he made the play!"

—Tom Paciorek

From 1988-1999, Paciorek, affectionately nicknamed "Wimpy," broadcast White Sox games. He was in the booth on September 30, 1990 when the White Sox defeated the Seattle Mariners 2-1. It was the final game played at the old Comiskey Park. His two quotes above came during the final inning of that game. Paciorek played eighteen years in the Majors compiling a lifetime .282 batting average. Playing for Seattle in 1981, Paciorek had his best season hitting .326. and was selected to the American League All-Star team. Paciorek also played for the Los Angeles Dodgers, Atlanta Braves, Chicago White Sox, New York Mets, and Texas Rangers.

Chapter Seven

All-Time
Chicago White Sox Greats

A baseball book covering a century of the team's players would not be complete without the effort of naming the all-time greats at each position. As you can imagine, this effort was not easy. Especially if you try to name no more than three players at each position, while at the same time naming five or six pitchers (from each side of the rubber) for your starting rotation and a handful of relievers to round out the list.

While doing research for this chapter, what helped me was information I had collected and kept over the years. In particular, I came across two lists that my brother, Don, and I had exchanged way back in 1992. We were talking about building a lineup to see if it could compete, all-time, against the mighty New York Yankees. Don is a sports buff, too, even more so than me. He has done a lot of reading and researching on sports, especially baseball and the Chicago White Sox. Back in 1992, we must have been having a conversation about who were the all-time greats for the Sox and on December 20th of that year, Don sent me a list of what he considered to be his top players in White Sox history. I countered a few days later with a list of my own. Granted, that was over twenty years ago and the White Sox have had some pretty special players don their uniform since. Guys like Paul Konerko and Chris

Sale, to name a couple. So, let's fast forward to 2017 to see what an All-Time Chicago White Sox Greats' Team would look like. Here's my list of Sox players who played at least five years on the South Side. Included are some statistics and personal comments. What might yours look like?

First Base:

Frank Thomas (Playing Career: 1990-2008; White Sox, 1990-2005) – The "Big Hurt" was by far the greatest offensive player in White Sox history. Sixteen of his nineteen years in the Big Leagues were spent banging out home runs and driving in runs in a Chicago uniform. Career stats: .301 Batting Average; 521 Home runs; 1,704 RBI; 2,468 Hits; back-to-back Most Valuable Player Award, 1993 and 1994; 5 All-Star appearances; received a 2005 World Series ring; his number 35 was retired by the White Sox on August 29, 2010; a statue of "Big Frank" was unveiled on the U.S. Cellular Field concourse in 2011; Thomas was admitted into the Hall of Fame on the first ballot in 2014.

Paul Konerko (Playing Career: 1997-2014; White Sox, 1999-2014) – "Paulie" is one of the all-time White Sox fan favorites. Sixteen of his eighteen years in the Major Leagues were spent with the White Sox. A professional hitter and fine first baseman, Konerko's career numbers should give him Hall of Fame consideration. Career stats: .279 Batting Average; 439 Home runs; 2,340 hits; 1,412 RBI; 6 All-Star appearances; his fielding average of .9952 ranks him 20th all-time defensively at first base; his uniform number 14 will eventually – and deservedly – be retired by the White Sox. Of note, Konerko caught the final out in the 2005 World Series game versus the Astros in Houston. He held onto the ball until the victory celebration and parade in downtown Chicago a few days later. At the podium, Konerko revealed the game ball and presented it to a surprised Jerry Reinsdorf, owner of the Chicago White Sox. Paul Konerko – class guy! Deservedly, "Paulie" had a statute portraying his grand slam homer versus the Houston Astros in the 2005 World Series unveiled in 2014.

Earl Sheely (Playing Career: 1921-1931; White Sox, 1921-1927) – Nicknamed "Whitey," Sheely played seven solid years with the White Sox from 1921-27. Playing on teams that had been decimated by the Black Sox scandal of 1919, Sheely never played for a first division team. However, his 1925 season garnered Most Valuable Player consideration in the American League, finishing sixth in the voting. Career stats: Batting Average .300; 1,340 Hits; Sheely was a solid player with over 600 plate appearances in six of his White Sox seasons, including 700 in 1925.

(Ineligible due to my arbitrary five-year minimum: Zeke Bonura and the great Dick Allen. Certainly, Jose Abreu has a chance to be one of the special ones at first base for the White Sox, too.)

Second Base:

Eddie Collins (Playing Career: 1906-1930; White Sox, 1915-1926) – One of the top all-time second basemen, Collins played twenty-five years in the Big Leagues, twelve of them with the White Sox. Collins started his career with Philadelphia, playing nine years with the Athletics, then came to the White Sox, and finally finished his amazing career back with the A's. Nicknamed "Cocky," Collins was considered one of the best all-around baseball players of all-time. Career stats: .331 Batting Average (26th all-time); 3,314 Hits (10th all-time); 741 career stolen bases (8th all-time); since 1900, Collins is one of only four Major League players with more than 500 stolen bases and a .400 on-base percentage; his .424 on-base percentage ranks Collins 11th all-time in the modern era; Most Valuable Player Award, 1914 (voted MVP either 2nd or 3rd four other times); four-time World Series Champion: 1910, 1911, 1913, and the White Sox in 1917); inducted into the Hall of Fame in 1939.

Nelson Fox (Playing Career: 1947-1965; White Sox, 1950-1963) – "Nellie" was a member of the "Go-Go" White Sox teams of the 50s and 60s. Fox was a key player both offensively and defensively during his fourteen years on the South Side, helping the White Sox to its first World Series in forty years. He was Mr. Dependable both at second base and batting second in the line-up. Career stats: Batting Average .288; 2,663 Hits; led the American League in hits in 1952, 1954, 1957, and 1958; led the American League in At-Bats in 1952, 1955, 1956, 1959, 1960; patrolling second base, Fox had a career .984 fielding average and won a Gold Glove three times; teamed with fellow Hall of Famer, Louie Aparicio, to form a solid double play combination from 1956-62; twelve time All-Star; named Most Valuable Player in the American League in 1959; Fox was admitted into the Hall of Fame in 1997. His uniform number 2 was retired in 1976. Fox and his double play partner, Aparicio, had statues unveiled together in 2005 on the concourse at U.S. Cellular Field.

Jorge Orta (Playing Career: 1972-1987; White Sox, 1972-1979) – A solid infielder who played eight of his sixteen years in baseball for Chicago, Orta was a versatile player, who played a variety of positions when called upon. Career stats: .278 Batting Average; 1,619 Hits; named as an All-Star twice.

Shortstop:

Luke Appling (Playing Career: 1930-1950; White Sox, 1930-1950) – Number 4 played his entire twenty-year career with the White Sox. These were lean years for the South Siders as they finished in the first division of the American League only four times. A fan favorite, Appling played through numerous injuries and was affectionately nicknamed "Old Aches and Pains." Career stats: .310 Batting Average; 2,749 Hits; led the American League in batting in 1936 and 1943 with a .388 and .310 batting average, respectively; seven time All-Star; Appling was admitted into the Hall of Fame in 1964. Luke's jersey number 4 was retired by the White Sox in 1975.

Louis Aparicio (Playing Career: 1956-1973; White Sox, 1956-1962 and 1968-1970) – Continuing the fine tradition of excellent shortstops, Aparicio played eighteen years in the Big Leagues, ten on the South Side. Louie was one of the leaders of the "Go-Go" White Sox, in the 1950s and 60s. Aparicio won Rookie of the Year honors in 1956. A slick fielder, "Little Louie" won nine Gold Gloves. One of the premier shortstops of his era, Aparicio was named to the American League All-Star team ten times. In 1959, he was runner-up in MVP voting to teammate and second baseman Nellie Fox. For seven years, they were the foundation for excellent defense up-the-middle, as well as double play combination. Career stats: .262 Batting Average; 2,677 Hits; Aparicio led the American League in steals nine straight years; "Little Louie" was admitted into the Hall of Fame in 1984. His uniform number 11 was retired by the White Sox in 1984. Aparicio and his double play partner, Nelson Fox, had statues unveiled together in 2005 on the concourse at U.S. Cellular Field.

Ozzie Guillen (Playing Career: 1985-2000; White Sox, 1985-1997) – Playing thirteen of his sixteen year Big League career on the South Side, Guillen sparkled at shortstop. He won the American League Rookie of the Year Award in 1985. He appeared in three All-Star games; Career stats: .264 Batting average; 1,764 Hits; although Number 13 is best known for managing the White Sox to the 2005 World Series, Ozzie was a solid player and deserves this all-time ranking.

Chico Carrasquel deserves honorable mention here as he played ten years in the Majors, six with the White Sox. George Davis does, too, as he was one of the best shortstops at the turn of the century – 20th century that is. The solid eight years Alexei Ramirez roamed the middle of the diamond for the White Sox gives him mention here in this category, too.

Third Base:

Robin Ventura (Playing Career: 1989-2004; White Sox, 1989-1998) – Third base is a key infield position, but also a power hitting one. Ventura's first ten years of his Major League career was with the White Sox. He was a solid fielder collecting five of his six Gold Gloves at the hot corner for Chicago. Career stats: .267 Batting Average; 1,885 Hits; 294 Home runs; 1,182 RBI; from 1990 through 1998, Ventura batted no lower than .262 and five times was a solid .282 or higher hitter.

Bill Melton (Playing Career: 1968-1977; White Sox, 1968-1975) – "Beltin Bill" was the first consistent home run hitter for the White Sox. In his eight years on the South Side, Melton homered 154 times and led the American League in 1971 in home runs with 33 – the first time a White Sox player had ever achieved this feat. Career stats: .253 Batting Average; 1,004 Hits; 160 Home runs.

Buck Weaver (Playing Career: 1912-1920; White Sox, 1912-1920) – This switch-hitter spent all nine of his years in the majors suiting up for Chicago and playing a total of 1,250 games. For the first four seasons Buck was at short, but starting in 1916, Weaver began playing more and more at third. Weaver's budding career was cut short due to the "Black Sox" scandal of 1919. From 1917 through his final year in 1920, Weaver batted .284, .300, .296, and .331, respectively. At age 29, Weaver was coming into his own as he approached his prime. Career stats: .272 Batting Average;

1,308 Hits. A potential Hall of Famer, Buck's career was cut short due to his being banned forever from baseball.

Joe Crede is right up there with a solid ten-year career – nine with the White Sox. Injuries cut short a promising career on the South Side. For Chicago fans, Crede will always be remembered as one of the heroes of the 2005 World Series Championship team.

Leftfield:

"Shoeless" Joe Jackson (Playing Career: 1908-1920; White Sox, 1915-1920) – During his brief Major League career that spanned thirteen years between the Philadelphia Athletics (2 years) and Cleveland Spiders (5½ years), Jackson played 5½ seasons for the Chicago White Sox. He was considered one of the premier hitters of his time. Jackson led the American League in hits both in 1912 and 1913 with 226 and 197, respectively. He led the league in triples three times in 1912, 1916, and 1920 with 26, 21, and 20, respectively. He also led the league in doubles with 39 in 1913. Since 1900, thirteen players have hit .400 or higher and Jackson is one of them. He batted .411 in 1911, but lost the batting title to Ty Cobb who batted .419. Jackson has the third best career batting average in the history of baseball with a .356 mark. Also known for his speed in the outfield, his fielding glove was known as "where triples go to die." Career stats: .356 Batting Average; 1,772 Hits, including 307 doubles and 168 triples (all-time White Sox leader); he was second in voting for the American League's Most Valuable Award in 1913. Destined for Cooperstown, "Shoeless" Joe's path to baseball immortality was derailed because of his role in the 1919 World Series scandal.

Minnie Minoso (Playing Career: 1949/1951 - 1964/ 1976/ 1980; White Sox, 1951 - 1957, 1960 - 1961, 1964, 1976, 1980) – One of the greats to don a White Sox uniform, Minnie is certainly the most popular player ever to play on the South Side of Chicago. Nicknamed the "Cuban Comet" and "Mr. White Sox," Minoso played three seasons for the New York Cubans in the Negro League before starting his Major League career with the Cleveland Indians in 1948. He was traded to the White Sox during the 1951 season. Ten of his seventeen years in the Big Leagues were spent with the White Sox. Minoso was the first black player to play for the Sox. Career stats: .298 Batting Average, 1,963 Hits; 186 Home runs; Minoso led the American League in triples in 1951, 1954, and 1956 with 14, 18, and 11, respectively; Minnie led the league in doubles legging out 36 in 1957; he used his speed to lead the American League in stolen bases in 1951, 1952, and 1953 with 31, 22, and 25, respectively; named to the American League All-Star team seven times; three-time Gold Glove award winner. Minoso was second in Rookie of the Year voting in 1951 when he batted .326, losing out to Yankee shortstop Gil McDougal who batted .306 that year. It should be noted that Minoso's numbers were better than McDougal's in all offensive areas except for home runs. Minoso's career spanned five decades starting when he first began playing in 1948 and then through the 1960s. Then, White Sox management allowed him to play in games in the 1970s and 1980s to become the only player to play in five decades. Minoso's number 9 jersey was retired in 1983 and he also deserves recognition and membership in the Hall-of-Fame. In 2004, a statue featuring Minnie was placed on the outfield concourse at U.S. Cellular Field.

Al Smith (Playing Career: 1953 - 1964; White Sox,1958 - 1962) – Acquired by the White Sox from the Cleveland Indians in 1958, Smith played five seasons for Chicago. Smith was a key player for the 1959 American League pennant winning team. Career stats: .272 Batting Average; 1,458 Hits; twice named to the American League All-Star team; a versatile player, Smith was valuable defensively, playing multiple positions in the infield and outfield. He played in two World Series: with Cleveland in 1954 and Chicago in 1959, both times ending up on the losing end.

Ron Kittle deserves honorable mention here playing eight of his ten Big League years for the White Sox.

Centerfield:

Jim Landis (Playing Career: 1957-1967; White Sox, 1957-1964) – Speedster and defensive star, Landis was a key member of the 1959 pennant winning "Go-Go" White Sox and a mainstay in his outfield position for eight years. He earned five Gold Glove awards, committing only 32 errors in 3,031 fielding chances. Career stats: .247 Batting Average; 1,061 Hits.

Happy Felsch (Playing Career: 1915-1920: White Sox, 1915-1920) – A very promising player, Felsch' six-year Big League career came to an abrupt end when he was banned from baseball following the 1919 Black Sox scandal. Felsch was an excellent fielder who possessed a strong throwing arm in center. Career stats: .293 Batting Average; 825 Hits; starred on the White Sox 1917 World Series Championship team and the 1919 White Sox America League pennant winner. Only time would tell if Felsch would have ended his playing days with an invitation to enter the Hall of Fame. If his first six years playing in the Majors was any indication of how he might have played out his career, entrance into Cooperstown might have awaited Happy Felsch.

Ken Berry (Playing Career: 1962-1975: White Sox, 1962-1970) – For nine of his fourteen years in the Major Leagues, Berry played on the South Side. He was a strong defensive outfielder who possessed speed while patrolling center. Berry committed only 30 errors while fielding 2,837 chances during his career. Career stats: .255 Batting Average; 1,053 Hits.

Chet Lemon deserves honorable mention here as does **Carl Reynolds.** Reynolds was extremely fast and at Comiskey Park actually raced against Yankee centerfielder Ben Chapman, on August 26, 1931. Chapman, who was considered the fastest player in baseball at the time, beat Reynolds in a 100 yard dash.

Rightfield:

Harold Baines (Playing Career: 1980-2001: White Sox, 1980-1989, 1996-1997, 2000-2001) – Playing fourteen of his twenty-two seasons on the South Side, Baines was a fan favorite. In Chicago, choruses of "Harold, Harold" could be heard whenever he approached the plate. Selected first in the first round of the 1977 amateur draft by the White Sox, Baines had a near Hall-of-Fame career playing outfield, as well as designated hitter. Career stats: .289 Batting Average; 2,866 Hits; 384 Home runs; 1,628 RBI; named six times to the American League All-Star team. Baines' uniform number 3 was retired by the White Sox in 1989 and Baines was honored by the franchise with a statue in 2008. It proudly stands in the outfield concourse. Hopefully, the Hall-of-Fame Veteran's Committee will eventually install "Harold, Harold" to his rightful place in Cooperstown.

Magglio Ordonez (Playing Career: 1997-2011; White Sox, 1997-2004) – For eight of his fifteen years in the Big Leagues, Ordonez played rightfield for the White Sox. A solid hitter, Magglio was a team leader with home runs and runs batted in. Injuries derailed a very promising career. Career stats: .309 Batting Average; 2,156 Hits; 294 Home runs; 1,236 RBI; named to the American League All-Star team six times; playing for the Detroit Tigers in 2007, Ordonez enjoyed his greatest season batting .363, leading the league with 54 doubles, and finishing second in Most Valuable Player balloting.

Jermaine Dye (Playing Career: 1996-2009: White Sox, 2005-2009) – Playing his final five years of his excellent career with the White Sox, Dye was voted the Most Valuable Player in the 2005 World Series. In Game 4 of the sweep of the Houston Astros, Jermaine singled in the lone run of the game. Dye batted .438 in the Fall Classic that included seven hits in sixteen official at-bats. He had one home run, one double, scored three times, and batted in three. Career stats: .274 Batting Average; 1,779 Hits; 325 Home runs; 1,072 RBI.

Walter "No Neck" Williams and **Carlos May** deserve honorable mention here as they were solid players for the White Sox. May was the first player to have his birthday printed on the back of his uniform: May 27. **Harry "Hoop" Hooper** also deserves honorable mention as he played the final five seasons of his seventeen-year Big League career patrolling the outfield for the White Sox.

Catcher:

Carlton Fisk (Playing Career: 1969-1993; White Sox, 1981-1993) – One of the premier backstops in baseball history, Fisk enjoyed thirteen of his twenty-four seasons behind the plate on the South Side. Nicknamed "Pudge" and "The Commander," Fisk was the first player to be named Rookie of the Year unanimously in 1972. He also won his lone Gold Glove award that year. Fisk received this distinction as a member of the Boston Red Sox where he spent the first eleven seasons of his career. Career stats: .269 Batting Average; 376 Home runs; 1,330 RBI; Fisk led the American League in triples with nine in his rookie season; voted to the American League All-Star team eleven times; on Tuesday 22, 1993, Fisk surpassed Bob Boone's record of games behind the plate with 2,226. His uniform number 72 was retired by the

White Sox in 1997. His number 27 was retired by the Boston Red Sox in 2000. Carlton Fisk was inducted into the Hall of Fame in 2000. A statue of "Pudge" was unveiled on the U.S. Cellular Field concourse in 2005.

Ray Schalk (Playing Career: 1912-1929; White Sox, 1912-1928) – The finest defensive catcher at the beginning of the Modern Era of baseball, Schalk played seventeen of his eighteen years in Chicago. He was also innovative at his position using speed and quickness to his advantage. He was a leader throughout his career and was a member of the 1917 Chicago White Sox World Series team. Although ending up on the losing side, Schalk was one of the stars of the 1919 World Series for the White Sox as he hit .304 reaching base twelve times in twenty-eight plate appearances. Career stats: .253 Batting Average; led the American League in throwing runners out attempting to steal a base in 1915, 1920, and 1925. Ray "Cracker" Schalk was inducted into the Hall of Fame in 1955.

Sherm Lollar (Playing Career: 1946-1963; White Sox, 1952-1963) – Playing twelve of his eighteen Big League seasons with the White Sox, Lollar was a mainstay behind the plate. An excellent defensive catcher, Lollar won four Gold Gloves. He also led the American League in throwing out base stealers in 1954. Known as the "Tank" for his slow foot speed, Lollar was a key member of the 1959 Chicago White Sox team that won the 1959 American League pennant for the first time in forty years. Career stats: .264 Batting Average; 155 Home Runs; 808 RBI; 1,415 Base Hits. Lollar made eight All-Star game appearances.

The incomparable **A.J. Pierzynski** deserves honorable mention here as one of the heroes of the 2005 World Series. A real gamer! He even knew how to steal first base!

Right-Handed Pitchers:

Ed Walsh (Playing Career: 1904-1917; White Sox, 1904-1916) – "Big Ed" was one of the greatest righthand pitchers in White Sox history. Playing thirteen of his fourteen Major League seasons with Chicago, Walsh compiled an impressive 195-125 record. Even more impressive was his 1.81 earned run average during that time. Walsh won forty games in 1908 while dropping fifteen. He was a workhorse on the mound. He lead the league in many pitching categories during his career: Lowest ERA in 1907 (1.60) and 1910 (1.27); Most Game Appearances in a season: 56 (1907), 66 (1908), 45 (1910), 56 (1911), and 62 (1912); Most Games Started in a season: 46 (1907), 49 (1908), and 41 (1912); Complete Games in a season: 37 (1907), and 42 (1908); Most Shutouts in a season: 10 (1906), 11 (1908), and 8 (1909); Innings Pitched in a season: 442.1 (1907), 464 (1908), 368.2 (1911), and 393 (1912); Most Strikeouts in a season: 269 (1908), and 255 (1911); Twice runner-up Most Valuable Player in the American League: 1911 and 1912. What makes Walsh's accomplishments so noteworthy is that he developed arm trouble in 1913 and won only thirteen in twenty-one decisions during his five final seasons. There is no pitcher in all of baseball at that time that was more dominant than "Big Ed" during the 1906 – 1912 seasons when he won 168 of his 195 total career wins. Walsh would have been a wonderful pitcher to see take the mound! He richly deserved enshrinement in the Hall of Fame. Walsh was inducted in 1946.

Urban Faber (Playing Career: 1914-1933: White Sox, 1914-1933) – "Red" Faber played his entire career toiling for the White Sox: 1914-1933. During his twenty-year career, Faber won 254 games while losing 213. Unfortunately, White Sox teams were over .500 only six times during that period. One of the heroes in the 1917 World Series, Faber won three games as Chicago claimed its second World Series title, four games to two, over the New York Giants. One can only imagine what Faber's career statistics might have been on better ball clubs, especially during the lean years from 1921 until his last season in 1933. For example, in 1921, the White Sox won only 62 games. Faber was on the hill for twenty-five of those victories. Afterwards, Faber never won more than fifteen games which he did in 1926. It's remarkable that during his twenty years pitching for the White Sox, "Red" Faber only had six losing seasons and two of them were during the final two seasons he played for Chicago in 1932 and 1933, going 2-11 and 3-4 respectively. Career stats: 254-213 Won-Loss Record; Career ERA: 3.15; Complete Games: 273; Lowest ERA in the American League: 2.48 (1921), and 2.81 (1922); Most Games Pitched in the American League: 50 (1915); Most Games Started in the American League: 39 (1920); Most Complete Games in the American League: 32 (1921), and 31 (1922); and Most Innings Pitched in the American League: 352 (1922). Urban "Red" Faber was inducted into the Hall of Fame in 1964.

Ted Lyons (Playing Career: 1923-1946; White Sox, 1923-1946) – Lyons career with the White Sox compares to that of "Red" Faber. Once again, Lyons' career spanned twenty-one years, all with the White Sox from 1923 to 1946. He won 260 games and lost 230. Lyons pitched on some fairly mediocre teams that were above .500 only six times. Yet, Lyons was the premier pitcher for the White Sox. For example, in 1925, Chicago's season record was only 66-87. Lyons went 21-11 that year and led the American League in victories. Two years later in 1927, the White Sox finished the season with a 70-83 record. Lyons once again led the league in wins when he recorded a 22-14 campaign on the mound. During his career, Lyons had only eight losing seasons for teams that didn't do well. Interestingly, as Lyons aged, he was used less frequently and White Sox Manager, Jimmy Dykes, decided to pitch him only on Sundays. Lyons earned the nickname "Sunday Teddy" as he won 52 games from 1939-1942. Career stats: 260-230 Won-Loss Record; Career ERA: 3.67; Complete Games: 356; Led the American League with Most Season Wins: 21 (1925) and 22 (1927); Most Complete Games in the American League: 30 (1927) and 29 (1930); Named to the American League All-Star team in1939. Inducted into the Hall of Fame in 1955.

Early "Gus" Wynn (Playing Career: 1939/1941-1944, 1946-1963: White Sox, 1958-1962) – The fourth righthanded starting pitcher to earn Hall of Fame recognition wearing the White Sox uniform was Early Wynn. Nicknamed "Gus," Wynn was a workhorse throughout his career achieving the magical 300 wins in 1963. During his twenty-three year career, Wynn played on two American League pennant winning clubs: The Cleveland Indians in 1954 that were swept by the New York Giants in the World Series and the Chicago White Sox who lost to the Los Angeles Dodgers in the 1959 World Series, 4 games to 2. In 1959, Wynn earned the American League Cy Young Award. Although Wynn pitched only five of his twenty-three seasons for the White Sox, he was always "Mr. Reliable" on the mound. Career stats: 300-244 Won-Loss Record; Career ERA: 3.54; Complete Games: 289; Most Wins in the American League: 23 (1954) and 22 (1959); Lowest ERA in the American League: 3.20 (1950); Led the American League in Games Started: 33 (1943), 34 (1951), 36 (1954), 37 (1957), and 37 (1959); Most Innings Pitched in the American League: 274.1 (1951), 270.2 (1954), and 255.2 (1959). Named to seven American League All-Star teams. Inducted into the Hall of Fame in 1972.

Left-Handed Pitchers:

Billy Pierce (Playing Career: 1945/1948-1964; White Sox, 1949 -1961) – One of the finest southpaws during his era, Pierce distinguished himself as an outstanding and consistent pitcher throughout his eighteen Big League seasons. Very dependable in big games, Billy played on two pennant winning clubs: The White Sox in 1959 when they lost to the Los Angeles Dodgers, four games to two, and then later in his career for the San Francisco Giants in 1962, losing to the New York Yankees in seven games. Career stats: 211-169 Won-Loss Record; Career ERA: 3.27; Complete Games: 193; Most Wins in the American League: 20 (1957); Led the American League in ERA: 1.97 (1955); Led the American League in Complete Games three straight years: 21 (1956), 16 (1957), and 19 (1958); Led the American League in Strikeouts: 186 (1953); Named to seven American League All-Star teams. Pierce's uniform number 19 was retired by the White Sox in 1987. A statue of Pierce was unveiled at U.S. Cellular Field in 2007. Someday, Billy Pierce deserves enshrinement in the Hall of Fame.

Mark Buehrle (Playing Career: 2000-2015; White Sox 2000-2011) – A fantastic pitcher for a dozen years on the South Side. Buehrle was one of the most consistent pitchers during his impressive career. Known as a fast worker on the mound, it was a fan's delight to see Number 56 pitch because when he had his tosses working for him – and that was the case in most appearances – it was not unreasonable to see a game last just a little over two hours. He pitched the ball. Got it back from his catcher and immediately was ready to fire another strike. Players defending behind Buehrle loved him for his workmanlike attitude. Besides his very efficient work habits, Buehrle hurled two no-hit games, including a perfect game on Thursday, July 23, 2009 defeating the Tampa Bay Rays, 5-0. Career stats: 214-160 Won-Loss Record; Career ERA: 3.81;

Most Games Started in a Season: 35 and 34 (2004, 2008); Named to five American League All-Star teams: 2002, 2005, 2006, 2009 (White Sox), 2014 (Toronto Blue Jays); Golden Glove Award (2009, 2010, 2011, 2012). Mark Buehrle: A real workhorse and deserving Hall of Fame consideration – and recognition! (As this book was being published, the White Sox announced that on June 24, 2017, the uniform number of Mark Buehrle will be retired. What an honor! Very justified. Congratulations Number 56!)

Guy "Doc" White (Playing Career: 1901-1913; White Sox, 1903-1913) – Although playing for the White Sox during the infancy of the American League, White was one of the dominant left-handed pitchers in the game during his eleven-year career for Chicago. During the 1901 and 1902 seasons, "Doc" pitched for the Philadelphia Phillies in the National League and recorded 14-13 and 16-20 seasons, respectively. For eight consecutive seasons on the South Side, White never had a losing season, winning seventeen, sixteen, seventeen, eighteen, twenty-seven (leading the American League in wins in 1907), eighteen, eleven, and fifteen games. He also led the American League with the lowest Earned Run Average in 1906 when he posted a remarkable 1.52 mark. "Doc" White was a workhorse. Career stats: 189-156 Won-Loss Record; Career ERA: 2.39; Complete Games: 262; Led the American League in ERA: 1.52 (1906); Most Wins in the American League: 27 (1907).

Tommy John (Playing Career: 1963-1974, 1975-1989; White Sox, 1965-1971) – This lefthander pitched for twenty-six years, seven with the White Sox. John had a remarkable career, one that some might say is deserving of a Hall of Fame plaque in Cooperstown. Yet, for all his success, the area everyone remembers this ballplayer for is the surgery that he received due to an arm injury in 1974. Carrying a 13-3 record, John permanently damaged his ulnar collateral ligament in his left arm while pitching for the Los Angeles Dodgers, John had performed on him – for the first time – a surgical procedure that took on his name: "Tommy John Surgery." John did not pitch the remainder of the season in 1974, as well as missed all of the 1975 season. When he returned to the mound, John was nearly unstoppable winning ten, twenty, seventeen, twenty-one, and twenty-two games over the next five years pitching for the Dodgers and New York Yankees. Career stats: 288-231 Won-Loss Record; Career ERA: Best Won-Loss Percentage in the National League: .696% in 1973 (16-7) and .813% in 1974 (13-3); Runner-up National League Cy Young Award: 1977 and 1979; Named four times to the All-Star team: 1968 (Chicago White Sox), 1978 (Los Angeles Dodgers), 1979 and 1980 (New York Yankees).

Wilbur Wood (Playing Career: 1961-1978; White Sox, 1967-1978) – Throwing a knuckleball, Wood dazzled batters for seventeen years, twelve with the White Sox. He was a workhorse and reminded fans of pitchers at the turn of the century. In 1973, Wood finished – and won – a 21 inning suspended game versus the Cleveland Indians when he completed the final two innings and was credited with the victory. He then pitched a complete game shutout in the regularly scheduled game, meaning he won two games in one day. Later that year, Wood started both ends of a doubleheader – the last time this feat has been attempted in the Major Leagues. Unfortunately, Wood came out on the losing end of both contests. Career stats: 164-156 Won-Loss Record; Career ERA: 3.24; Most Wins in the American League: 24 (1972 and 1973); Most Games Appeared in a Season: 88, 76, and 77 (1968, 1969, and 1970); Most Games Started in a Season: 49, 48, 42, and 43 (1972, 1973, 1974, and 1975); Most Complete Games in a Season: 46 (1968) and 62 (1970); Most Innings Pitched in a Season: 376.2 (1972) and 359.1 (1973); Runner-up American League Cy Young Award: 1972; Named to three American League All-Star teams.

Chris Sale (Playing Career: 2010-2016; White Sox, 2010-2016) – As this book was being published, southpaw Sale, definitely the ace of the White Sox pitching staff, as well as one of the best pitchers throwing from either side in baseball was traded to the Boston Red Sox. Beginning in the bullpen during the 2010 season, Sale distinguished himself in the starting rotation in 2012. Ever since, number 49 was named to the American League All-Star team. At age 27, barring injury, Sale may well on his way to not only 300 wins, but also a place in the Hall of Fame. There, he would join other illustrious hurlers who toiled on the mound. Also, Sale should continue to be considered as a Cy Young candidate. Career stats (as of 2016 season): 74-50 Won-Loss Record; Career ERA: 3.00; Named to five American League All-Star teams.

Five other southpaws deserving honorable mention are **Thornton Lee** who pitched eleven of his sixteen years in the Big Leagues with the White Sox (1937-1947) achieving a 117-124 record; **Reb Russell** who had a seven-year Major League career with the White Sox (1913-1919) and pitched on the 1917 World Series and 1919 American League pennant clubs. Russell took the mound 52 times in 1913 when he recorded a 22-16 record – unfortunately, injuries took their toll on a very promising career; **Juan Pizarro** toiled eighteen years in the Majors winning 131 while losing 105 games. "Wonderful Juan" pitched six years on the South Side and appeared in two American League All-Star games (1963, 1964); **Gary Peters** won 124 and lost 103 games in a fourteen-year career – 11 with the Pale Hose and was named to the American League All-Sar team in 1964 and 1967; **Claude**

Williams pitched five of his seven Big League years for the White Sox (1916-1920). "Lefty" had an overall 82-48 career record. His promising career was cut short due to his involvement in the 1919 Black Sox scandal.

Right-Handed Relief Pitchers:

Hoyt Wilhelm (Playing Career: 1952-1972; White Sox, 1963-1968) – Nicknamed "Old Tilt" for the way he slanted his head while gazing in for the catcher's signal, Wilhelm dazzled batters in a relief career that earned him Hall of Fame enshrinement. Hoyt began his career late, as a starting pitcher for the New York Giants at age 29. However, it was decided that his knuckleball was more conducive for short appearances in a game. He pitched for twenty-one years, mostly in relief. He won 124 games coming out of the bullpen. Wilhelm was also the first pitcher to record 200 saves. Due to his longevity, he was the first pitcher to appear in 1,000 games. Career stats: 143-122 Won-Loss Record; Career ERA: 2.52; Lowest ERA in the National League: 2.43 (New York Giants, 1952); Lowest ERA in the American League: 2.19 (Baltimore Orioles, 1959); Most Games Appeared in a Season: 71 and 68 (1952 and 1953); Second in voting for Rookie of the Year in the National League (1952); Named to five All-Star teams: 1953 (New York Giants), 1959, 1961 and 1962 (Baltimore Orioles)and 1970 (Atlanta Braves and Chicago Cubs). Inducted into the Hall of Fame in 1985.

Rich "Goose" Gossage (Playing Career: 1972-1994: White Sox, 1972-1976) – Gossage played the first five of his twenty-two year Big League career with the White Sox. "Goose" became one of the premier relief pitchers performing his lights-out duties for nine teams. Career stats: 124-107 Won-Loss Record; Career ERA: 3.01; Led the American League in Most Saves in a Season: 26, 27, and 33 (1975, 1978, and 1980); Named to nine All-Star teams: 1975 and 1976 (Chicago White Sox), 1977 (Pittsburgh Pirates), 1978, 1980, 1981, and 1982 (New York Yankees), 1984 and 1985 (San Diego Padres). Inducted into the Hall of Fame in 2008.

Bobby Thigpen (Playing Career: 1986-1994; White Sox, 1986-1993) – Playing eight of his nine years on the South Side, Thigpen was a saves machine. In 1990, he set the record for most saves in a season recording 57 opportunities. Career stats: 31-36 Won-Loss Record; Career ERA: 3.43; Most Games Pitched in a Season: 77 (1990); Most Games Finished in a Season: 59 and 73 (1988 and 1990); Most Saves in a Season: 57 (1990); Named to one American League All-Star team (1990).

Keith Foulke and **Bobby Jenks** deserve honorable mention.

Lefthanded Relief Pitchers:

Matt Thornton (Playing Career: 2004-2016; White Sox, 2006-2013) – Southpaw Thornton spent the middle portion of his Major League career with the White Sox. He was one of the most dependable short relief pitchers in the game and was often called upon to shut down an uprising by getting a specific out in a close late inning game using his lights-out fastball. Career stats: 36-46 Won-Loss Record; Career ERA: 3.36; Appeared in 63, 68, 74, 70, 61, 62, 74, 40 games for the White Sox (2006-2013); Named to one All-Star team (2010).

Terry Forster (Playing Career: 1971-1986; White Sox, 1971-1976) – For sixteen seasons, Forster hurled for five Major League teams. He began his career with the White Sox and quickly became the "go-to" guy in the bullpen. Career stats: 54-65 Won-Loss Record; 3.23 Career ERA; Led the American League in Saves: 24 (1974).

Managers:

Al Lopez – A sturdy backstop who had an excellent Big League playing career, Lopez enjoyed much success as a manager. Playing nineteen years for the Brooklyn Dodger, Boston Bees, Pittsburgh Pirates, and Cleveland Indians, Lopez set the record for most games catching at 1,918 upon his retirement as a player in 1947 – which stood for forty years. Known as "El Señor" (The Gentleman), Lopez was selected as the manager for the Cleveland Indians in 1951. He took the Tribe to the World Series in 1954 only to see his team swept by the New York Giants. From 1957 to 1965, Lopez was the skipper for the White Sox. He returned for brief stints in that position during the 1968-1969 seasons. White Sox fans remember Lopez for leading the 1959 team to the American League pennant, winning 94 games while dropping sixty. The "Go-Go" White Sox were an exciting team displaying excellent defense, timely hitting and solid pitching. Lopez handled his players well and in return they respected his judgment and leadership. The White Sox faced the Los Angeles Dodgers in the 1959 World Series, losing four games to two. Career stats (Player): .261 Batting Average; 1,547 Hits; voted twice to the National League All-Star team: 1934 (Brooklyn Dodgers) and 1941 (Pittsburgh Pirates). Career stats (Manager): 1,410-1,004 Won-Loss Record, 570-354 (Cleveland Indians) and 840-650 (Chicago White Sox) – 26th all-time. Lopez managed two American League pennant winners: 1954 (Cleveland Indians) and 1959 (Chicago White Sox). Inducted into the Hall of Fame as a Manager in 1977.

Ozzie Guillen – Number 13 was a star shortstop, and later star manager for the South Side. Best known for his leading the White Sox to their first World Series in 88 years as their manager, Guillen is also remembered for his playing days. In 1985, Ozzie was named Rookie of the Year in the American League when he led the

Mark's most favorite and most read book – the 1963 edition of The Official Encyclopedia of Baseball compiled by Hy Turkin and S.C. "Tommy" Thompson. It was given to him by his dad that year who signed it as "Stan Musial." Shortly thereafter, Mark learned that it was my dad's handwriting. For Mark, this is priceless. The tenth edition of *The Encyclopedia of Baseball* is also one of his favorites.

junior circuit in fielding as a shortstop with a .980 fielding percentage. Also, Guillen was named to three All-Star teams. He played thirteen years for the White Sox before moving on to play for the Baltimore Orioles for one year before completing his playing career with the Atlanta Braves. Career stats (Player): .264 Batting Average; 1,764 Hits; voted three times to the American League All-Star team (1988, 1990, 1991). Career stats (Manager): 747-710 Won-Loss Record, 678-617 (Chicago White Sox) and 69-93 (Miami Marlins). Guillen managed the White Sox to the 2005 World Series sweeping the Houston Astros in four games. During the 2005 playoffs, the White Sox won eleven of their twelve post-season games. That year, Guillen was named Manager of the Year.

William "Kid" Gleason – Compiling a .519 won-loss percentage at the helm of the White Sox, Gleason began his five-year tenure taking Chicago to its third World Series appearance. Unfortunately, several players of his fine team were implicated in a scandal to throw the World Series versus the Cincinnati Reds. Gleason also had a long playing career as a pitcher and fielder in twenty-two seasons beginning in 1888 and ending in 1912. Beginning in 1888, Gleason played for the Philadelphia Quakers, Philadelphia Phillies, St. Louis Browns, Baltimore Orioles, New York Giants, Detroit Tigers, and Chicago White Sox. Career stats (Player): 138-131 Won-Loss Pitching Record; .261 Batting Average; 1,946 Hits; one of twenty-nine baseball players to play in four decades. Career stats (Manager): 759-392 Won-Loss Record; Gleason was the man in charge of the American League pennant winning White Sox team that lost to Cincinnati in the 1919 World Series five games to three. The 1919 Sox season record was 88-52.

Jimmy Dykes – His long baseball career included twenty-two years playing and twenty-one as manager. As an infielder and at the plate, Dykes was a dependable player for fifteen years with the Philadelphia Athletics and then completed his career with the White Sox where he played for seven years. Career stats (Player): .280 Batting Average; 2,256 Hits. Career stats (Manager): 1,406-1,541 Won-Loss Record, 899-940 (Chicago White Sox), 208-254 (Philadelphia Athletics), 54-100 (Baltimore Orioles), 24-17 (Cincinnati Redlegs), 118-115 (Detroit Tigers), and 103-115 (Cleveland Indians). Dykes was the player-manager for the White Sox from 1934 to 1939.

Tony La Russa deserves honorable mention as he spent eight of his thirty-three year managerial career with the White Sox. La Russa was also inducted into the Hall of Fame in 2014. **Clarence "Pants" Rowland,** who directed the White Sox to their best season ever in 1917, and **Chuck Tanner** are very worthy of recognition as skippers for the Chicago White Sox.

"I used to try not to lose before. Now, when I go out, I go out to win every time, and I'm certain I am. I try to envision myself literally walking off the mound a winner. I allow no negatives in my thinking. When certain ones start creeping in, I erase them and make it like a blank blackboard waiting to be filled in with things like, 'The team is going to play well, is going to score some runs, I'm going to throw strikes, I'm going to win.'"

(Regarding his pitching career, 1980)

—Steve Stone

One of baseball's foremost analysts, Stone has announced White Sox games since 2008. His Big League pitching career spanned eleven years hurling for the San Francisco Giants, Chicago White Sox, Chicago Cubs, and Baltimore Orioles. Stone was the American League Cy Young Award winner in 1980, posting a Major League best 25-7 mark with the Baltimore Orioles.

7th Inning

LAST GAME AT OLD COMISKEY PARK

Who can forget their first baseball game? But, how many people can remember the last game played at their favorite ballpark?

As a lifelong fan, I had gone to many Sox games at the Old Comiskey Park. The field was built in 1910 by the owner and founder of the White Sox, Charles Comiskey, better known as "The Old Roman." The park he built took on the features of an old Roman Coliseum with its portals for windows. Many great players had graced Comiskey Park over its long and illustrious history. Great White Sox players like "Shoeless" Joe Jackson, Urban "Red" Faber, "Old Aches and Pains" Luke Appling, Early "Gus" Wynn, Sherman "Tank" Lollar, Orestes "Minnie" Minoso, to name just a few. Plus, a couple of my own personal favorites as I was growing up. Guys like Mike Herschberger, a fine-fielding rightfielder who had a strong accurate arm that gunned down many a runner trying to score or take an extra base. "Iron Mike" wore number 40 and was an average hitter, but I followed him in his short career with the White Sox. Or, right-handed pitcher, Ray Herbert. People said I looked like Herbert so I took to liking number 21 and followed his career with the Sox. Good, steady pitcher.

There were a number of great players who visited Comiskey Park over the years wearing opposing uniforms. Yankees' Babe Ruth, Lou Gehrig, Joe DiMaggio, Mickey Mantle, and Yogi Berra to name a few of the Bronx Bombers. The Red Sox' Ted Williams, Tigers' Ty Cobb, and Hank

Greenberg, Senators' Walter "Big Train" Johnson, Indians' Lou Boudreau, and Harvey Kuehn, Browns' (and later Orioles) Brooks Robinson, and Jim Palmer, and the Twins' Harmon "Killer" Killebrew and Rod Carew, to name just a few.

But wait! How many people know that before Jackie Robinson broke the color line in 1947, several stars of the Old Negro Leagues played before throngs of fans at Comiskey Park? These stars included Satchel Paige, Josh Gibson, "Cool Papa" Bell, and Buck Leonard. In fact, the East-West Negro League All-Star games were almost exclusively played in Comiskey Park.

Yes, Comiskey Park was the sight of many great ball clubs and players who took the field over its eighty-year history. In 1933, Comiskey was selected to host the first All-Star Game that was won by the American League and featured Babe Ruth hitting the first home run in All-Star Game history.

Yet as my father-in-law, Jerry, would say, "Everything has a beginning and everything has an end." And so the same was true for Comiskey Park as the White Sox were slated to move into their new home adjacent to the old for the start of the 1991 season.

My brother, Don, his boys, and our son, Stephen, and I got tickets for the first game of the final series at Old Comiskey Park in September 1990. The four game series featured the Seattle Mariners coming to town to bring down the curtain on Comiskey. We wanted to be a part of Chicago baseball history so we bought tickets for the Thursday night game. Driving from Milwaukee where we lived, we got there early to take in the nostalgia of this great landmark on Chicago's South Side. Before the game, we

(On the facing page) On Sunday, September 30, 1990, the curtain closed on Comiskey Park! Our family was there as the game ended to soak up the atmosphere, nostalgia, and memories of great players and games played at "The Palace." One of the items we bought outside the entrance was a poster of the great "Shoeless" Joe Jackson. The collector's shirt was a surprise gift presented to Mark over a quarter century later in 2016 by an old Northern Illinois University buddy, Jack Simpson. How thoughtful!

wound our way around the park – starting from the home plate area, down the left field line, first behind the Sox dugout, and then towards the left field foul pole. Eventually, we found ourselves in the picnic area under the left field grandstand looking at ground level behind a screen at batting practice taking place. To our surprise, who came up to greet us? One of the all-time White Sox greats – Minnie Minoso! He was impeccably dressed in a dress suit that fit him like a glove, along with his trademark warm, infectious, and ever-present smile. We enjoyed meeting Minnie and asked him a few questions and, of course, his autograph. He politely obliged our every request. What a gentleman! Minnie asked our first names as he signed our programs. What a special moment that was for all of us, but especially for my brother and me, because we had grown up with number 9 always hustling in left field or on the base paths after hitting a double or triple. He was one of the greatest White Sox players of all-time. Minoso was also the first black player on the Sox who played from 1949 to 1980 - five decades! Unfortunately, he missed playing on the 1959 Sox pennant team as he was dealt to the Cleveland Indians for the '58 season. Ironically, Minnie returned to Chicago in 1960 and played for a very good team that went 87-67. Deserving to be in the Hall of Fame, I eventually hope Minoso gets elected by the Veterans Committee. His superb career definitely warrants it! Minoso certainly was a Hall of Famer on that special September night as the curtain was closing on Old Comiskey.

After meeting Minoso, we continued our journey: scaling the catwalk behind the exploding scoreboard and over to the right field stands and back down the right field line to our seats behind the first base dugout. We wanted to be able to see our favorite team's dugout so we could catch a glimpse of the players as they took the field or returned to the dugout after playing it or got ready to pick up a bat to approach home plate. The outcome of the game saw the White Sox losing 7-3, but it seemed secondary to the fact that we were witnessing the passing of a great and historic ballpark.

After returning to Milwaukee after the game, we made a stop at one of our favorites: Superdawg on Milwaukee Avenue. There's nothing like a Superdawg and a chocolate shake, regardless if your team has won or lost. Superdawg is a winner!

Interestingly, our family drove back to Chicago for the weekend to visit my parents and in-laws. Both lived about a mile apart near Midway Airport. However, one thing we did as a family as we began our drive back to Wisconsin on that Sunday afternoon was to plan a stop at Comiskey. We wanted to be around the park after the final out to see and be a part of the closing of "The Place." I listened to the game on the radio and we planned our departure from my wife's parents' home close to the end of the game that was won by our White Sox, 2-1. We packed up the kids in our car and sped over to Comiskey. We parked our car just as fans were exiting the park and we began to mill about the vendors hawking souvenirs.

We all absorbed the moment! The happy faces. The sad faces. Fans who had seen not only a season-ending home game, but also experiencing the curtain falling on a great ballpark. History was being made nonetheless. We searched for souvenirs, something that we could take home with us to remember this special day. I found a street vendor who was selling pennants, caps, and tee-shirts. But, something caught my eye! A poster of "Shoeless" Joe Jackson! I bought one – and still have it – with memories of a great ballplayer, a great franchise, and a great ballpark. By the way, the Jackson poster is really cool. It shows Jackson snaring a fly ball in the outfield with his famous glove known as "the glove where triples go to die."

What a weekend I had! And I'm glad that on this final day of Comiskey Park's long career of hosting many, many historic games and events that my three kids, Michelle, Karen, and Steve, along with my wife, Ann, were there with me to enjoy and relish this special moment together - forever!

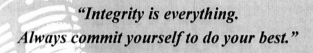

*"Integrity is everything.
Always commit yourself to do your best."*

Darrin Jackson

After Jackson's eleven-year playing career, including two different years on the South Side in 1994 and 1999, he has broadcast White Sox games beginning in 2000 to the present. Jackson patrolled the outfield twelve years with the Chicago Cubs, San Diego Padres, Toronto Blue Jays, New York Mets, Minnesota Twins, Milwaukee Brewers, and Chicago White Sox.

Chapter Eight

My Favorite White Sox Players...and Yours?

What baseball fan does not have a favorite player – or two or three or more – that they follow and root for during the season? Some favorites are short-lived while others are thought of fondly throughout their careers or even longer.

Growing up, I had several White Sox favorite players. While I share mine, I hope you will think of your own. I know they will bring up wonderful memories. They do for me!

The 1950s and 60s had so much going on for me. I was growing up! While doing so, I was fortunate to be able to do lots of things that still bring back some great memories. We didn't have a lot of money, but my parents made sure that we never felt we were missing anything. Besides, we lived in neighborhoods with lots of other families and kids that shared the common experience of growing up after the Second World War. Our parents worked. We went to school and played outside every chance we got. We rarely went on vacations and a drive to our grandparents' house on the North Side on a Sunday afternoon after church was a big thing. Once in a while, we got a special treat – having a fun day at Riverview Amusement Park. That was a real treat and anyone who experienced a day riding the rollercoasters (my favorites were the Greyhound and Fireball), or sailing down the slide of the Chutes to Chutes and hoping to get soaking wet, or riding the melodious Merry-Go-Round will always remember that landmark. There's something magical about Riverview that I wish my own kids and grandchildren could experience.

My parents treated my brothers and me to a White Sox game maybe once or twice a summer. They'd pack a few sandwiches and off we'd go to Comiskey. We'd sit in the grandstand, watch the game, listen to the organ music try to rev up the crowd – my favorite was: "The sun shines east, the sun shines west, deep in the heart of Texas." Looking back, I wonder what that had to do with being at a ballgame in Chicago, but it was a catchy tune so I remember it well. My parents would spring for a soda and popcorn to go with the packed sandwiches. We'd sit back, talk about the game, and just enjoy the experience regardless if the White Sox won or lost. In fact, I can't remember the final scores of many of those games, but I do remember what a beautiful experience it was to be at a ballgame with my parents. It was really a family affair.

During the late 1950s and early 60s, I grew to having some special players that I still remember today. For example, someone told me that I resembled right-handed pitcher Ray Herbert. I got his baseball card and I guess there was a resemblance somewhere, but old number 21 still became one of my favorites. Herbert had a fourteen-year Major League career and won 104 games while dropping 107. During his four years with the White Sox (1961-64), Herbert was 48-32. He won 20 games and lost only nine in 1962 when he was named to the All-Star team. Another player that I liked was right-fielder "Iron Mike" Hershberger. I'm not sure why. Maybe it was because I sometimes played right field on my Little League team and imagined being number 40 catching a fly ball to end a game. Hershberger played eleven seasons – the first four with the White Sox (1961-64) and his final year in the Big Leagues (1971). He had a respectable .252 batting average. But, he was most known for his defense and strong arm in right. Does Harry "Suitcase" Simpson ring any bells for the reader? Simpson was a journeyman outfielder and first baseman during his eight-year Big League career. He was also one of the first African-American players to play in the American League. He only played in 33 games as a utility man and pinch hitter for the White Sox in 1959, but he still remains one of those favorites of mine. New York Yankee Manager Casey Stengel thought a lot about "Suitcase," too. Stengel once said that Simpson was one of the best defensive right fielders in the American League.

What kid growing up in Chicago during the 1950s can't remember the Go-Go White Sox teams? These were special years for me growing up on the South Side and being a White Sox fan made it even more so. As a result, the names and numbers of the '59 American League Champion White Sox are imbedded forever in my mind: Luis Aparacio at shortstop (Number 11), Nelson "Nellie" Fox at second (Number 2), Jim Landis in center (Number 1), Sherm Lollar behind the plate (Number 10), Norm Cash at first (Number 38), Al Smith in right or left field (Number 16), Johnny Callison playing rightfield (Number 9), and Bubba Phillips at third (Number 5), plus pitchers Early "Gus" Wynn (Number 24), Billy Pierce (Number 19), Dick Donovan (Number 22), Barry Latman (Number 18), Bob Shaw (Number 35), Turk Lown (Number 27), and Gerry Staley (Number 21). There's a whole bunch more, too. Like utility man Sammy Esposito (Number 14), and Ted Kluzewski at first base (Number 8) who fortunately joined the team mid-season. "Big Klu" also hit two home runs in the first game of the 1959 World Series along with five RBIs as the White Sox hammered the Los Angeles Dodgers at Comiskey Park, 11-0. Billy Goodman at third (Number 6), Earl Torgeson at first (Number 17), catchers Earl Battey (Number 26) and John "Honey" Romano (Number 20). I can't forget Jim McAnany in right (Number 3). Who can forget

Manager Al Lopez? "El Señor" led the White Sox during their crucial growing years helping the players – and fans – believe that a pennant was possible after so many lean years. His long and distinguishing career as a catcher - combined with his outstanding managerial leadership - entitled him entrance to the Hall of Fame. Lopez's number? 42. There's others, too. I've thought about these players throughout my lifetime. I wonder if they knew the impact they had on that little kid growing up in Chicago?

Certainly through the years, I've grown to love other players. My all-time favorite? Frank Thomas. The "Big Hurt" brought such joys to the South Side as he banged the ball as one of the most feared hitters in all of baseball. His Hall of Fame career makes Number 35 most definitely the greatest offensive player in the history of the franchise. He certainly deserved being named to the Hall on the first ballot. Another first baseman that I grew to love watching was Paul Konerko. One of the heroes of the White Sox 2005 World Series Championship team, "Paulie" had a fantastic career! His quiet leadership was an enduring quality that made him a fan favorite. Although slow afoot, Konerko was a clutch hitter and a very solid defensive first sacker. Konerko's 439 career home runs place him second only to Thomas on the all-time White Sox list in this category. Captain Paulie is one of the all-time Sox players and not just one of my favorites. He's definitely on that special list White Sox fans throughout the world admire.

For me, those White Sox players on the 1917 and 1919 teams stick with me as favorites, too. "Shoeless" Joe Jackson, one of the greatest players of his time, deserves to be seen as a fan favorite not only for me, but other fans, too. This is not to ignore what he was accused of doing during the 1919 World Series. Being implicated in the worst scandal ever to take place in baseball is nothing to look past, but you also can't ignore the tremendous player Jackson was.

Not only was he a superb hitter – his .356 lifetime batting average still ranks number three all-time – but he was also fast, making him a fantastic outfielder. Think about these statistics and how they attest to Jackson's speed and keen eye at the plate: in 1920, "Shoeless" Joe had 20 triples and only 14 strikeouts as he recorded a .382 batting average! He was some kind of baseball player!

For some reason, I have come to the realization that the 1919 Black Sox scandal ruined the careers of some promising ballplayers. Still, I am drawn to the greatness and potential greatness of some of those White Sox players. For me, Eddie Cicotte definitely had a Hall of Fame career. Happy Felsch was establishing himself as a great centerfielder and hitter. Might Felsch found himself in the Hall? I definitely think so. Buck Weaver was already known as a slick fielder and fan favorite by 1919, but he also showed some excellent hitting strengths during the 1920 season batting .331 in 151 games. Weaver's .272 lifetime batting average looked to improve in subsequent years. What might have been no one knows for sure, but I think Weaver had the potential for Hall of Fame consideration. Claude "Lefty" Williams was another. He should be considered one of the all-time White Sox pitchers because in seven years he already had an extremely respectable won-loss ratio: 82-48 that included 80 complete games. He was only 27 years old when he was banished forever from baseball. What might have been?

Others on that team that I always looked back on with fond memories of a White Sox dynasty in the making were Eddie Collins, "Red" Faber, and Ray Schalk – all Hall of Famers. They changed the game by playing it in exemplary fashion. Collins with his speed, hitting, and long career; Schalk with his unique style at the catcher's position, and Faber with pitching brilliance. Collins, nicknamed "Cocky," played 25 years and during his career amassed

3,315 hits along with his .333 batting average. One of baseball's greats at second base. Catcher Schalk revolutionized the backstop position by being much more involved with the defense. For example, he was the first catcher to back-up plays at first base. He used his speed in other ways, too. In 1916, he set the record for most steals by a catcher (30) that stood until 1982. Known as "The Cracker," Schalk played 17 of his 18-year career with the White Sox. A great one! While doing research for this book, I began to better appreciate the career of Urban "Red" Faber who was one of the heroes of the 1917 World Series. Faber won three games and pitched in four of the six games. He's also in the Hall of Fame – and deservedly so.

Although I never saw "Big Ed" Walsh pitch, I have read enough to appreciate what a tremendous ballplayer he was. Can you imagine winning 40 games in a season? Walsh accomplished this feat in 1908, winning forty and losing fifteen games. His overall career record was 195-126 and in fourteen years on the mound for the White Sox, he had a 1.82 ERA. Yes, Ed Walsh is enshrined in the Hall of Fame.

Luke Appling was one of the many players White Sox fans enjoyed patrolling the infield at shortstop. His .310 lifetime batting average over a twenty-year playing career from 1930-1950 earned "Old Aches and Pains" (who played through injuries throughout his career, thus his nickname) enshrinement in the Hall of Fame.

Jump to the 1980s and I can picture Number 72 behind the plate. Carlton Fisk reversed his jersey number when he came to the White Sox from the "other" Sox team. Wearing his signature "72" on the back of his Chicago uniform, "Pudge" played thirteen of his twenty-four Big League seasons with the White Sox. When Fisk retired, he held the records for most home runs as a catcher (351) and games caught (2,226). These records have since been surpassed.

However, there is no doubt Carlton Fisk is one of the greatest catchers in baseball history. "The Commander" Fisk played the majority of his career in Chicago and was enshrined into the Hall of Fame in 2000.

There have been so many White Sox players that I have been privileged to watch either in person, or most likely on television, or simply listening on the radio. They have brought so much interest and joy to my life. I certainly can't close this chapter without mentioning players like Harold Baines whose 2,866 all-time hits over a 21-year career certainly deserves consideration for admittance into the Hall of Fame. I believe he will make it down the line because "Harold" was a great hitter and a fan favorite throughout his White Sox career. That's one of the reasons a statute honoring Number 3 stands on the concourse at 35th and Shields.

I can't forget to mention other players I grew up with – guys like pitchers Joel Horlen, Gary Peters, Wilbur Wood, and Hoyt Wilhelm. I never saw Hall of Famer Ted Lyons pitch, but winning 260 while losing 230 games for some losing ball clubs, warranted enshrinement. A real fan favorite, Lyons became known as "Sunday Teddy" in 1942 because Manager Jimmy Dykes decided to use the right-hander exclusively on Sunday as a drawing card. "Teddy" responded by completing all of his twenty starts while compiling a 14-6 record.

There are many deserving players who donned the White Sox uniform from 1917 through 2016. The "Go-Go White Sox" of the 1950s and 60s – when "my" era of watching Chicago White Sox baseball truly began in earnest – ignited my love affair with my South Side heroes. A love that has only grown through the years!

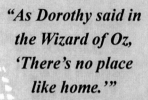

"As Dorothy said in the Wizard of Oz, 'There's no place like home.'"

—Ed Farmer

Farmer has been a member of the White Sox broadcasting team for twenty-five years. An eleven-year Major League pitcher, Farmer spent the 1979-1981 seasons with the White Sox. In 1980, Farmer set a White Sox record for saves in a season with 30. He was also named to the American League All-Star team that year. Besides the White Sox, Farmer pitched for the Cleveland Indians, Detroit Tigers, Philadelphia Phillies, Baltimore Orioles, Milwaukee Brewers, Texas Rangers, and Oakland Athletics.

8th Inning

GREAT CHISOX BACKSTOPS

Who is the greatest catcher in White Sox history? I'm sure some will add a name or two to my list, but for me, three catchers stand out with Carlton Fisk needing to be considered the best in the history of the franchise.

Although Fisk went into the Hall of Fame wearing a Red Sox cap, "Pudge" played more seasons for the White Sox and broke the all-time record for games as a catcher in 1993 while with the Pale Hose.

Certainly, Hall of Famer Ray Schalk, who played in a much different era, still deserves to be on any all-time catcher list, as he led the White Sox to a World Series Championship in 1917 over the New York Giants, four games to two. "Cracker" was also behind the plate in 1919 as a member of the team that won the pennant, but lost to the Cincinnati Reds in the Black Sox scandal, five games to three. A solid hitter, Schalk was one of the finest defensive backstops, especially during the early years of baseball.

Sherman Lollar was a fine catcher for the Sox in the late 1950s and early '60s. A fine hitter, especially in the clutch, Sherm was superb at calling games. And, he had some terrific hurlers to call signals for: Hall of Famer Early "Gus" Wynn, Hall of Fame wannabee (and shouldabee) Billy Pierce, plus Dick Donavan, Barry Latman, Bob Shaw, Juan Pizarro, Gary Peters, and Joe Horlen.` Lollar's one drawback was his speed — or lack thereof. That's why he got the nickname "Tank" because he ran the bases at a very slow pace. An example of this took place in the bottom of the eighth inning of the second game of the 1959 World Series with the White Sox holding a 1-0 Series lead over the Los Angeles Dodgers. Lollar was thrown out at the plate as he tried to score from first base on a double by Al Smith. A faster runner would have scored, but "Tank" didn't and the Sox went on to lose the game and Series, four games to two. Lollar's lack of speed does not disqualify him as being one of the top Sox catchers ever. Finally, who can leave off the list of great Sox receivers but none other than A.J. Pierzynski? In 2005, he led the Sox to their first World Series Championship in 88 years! A.J. is a gamer. He knows how to play the game and is a player who you either love – when he plays for your team – or hate – if he's wearing the opposing uniform. Pierzynski definitely deserves mention on the all-time catcher's list for the White Sox.

On a beautiful and warm summer evening, Tuesday, June 22, 1993, Carlton Fisk would make baseball history by catching in what was at the time the most games at that position, 2,226 games. He broke the record held by Bob Boone, which was held previously by Al Lopez, former Cleveland Indians' catcher who later went on to manage the Indians and White Sox.

Fisk's record-breaking game was to be played at the new Comiskey Park versus the Texas Rangers. I thought, "Wouldn't it be fun to be part of baseball history?" As it turned out, our son, Stephen, was playing YMCA catch-pitch baseball near our home in Wauwatosa, Wisconsin that evening at 6:00 p.m. Also, our oldest daughter, Michelle, had been spending a long weekend at her grandparents' house on the South Side of Chicago. I mentioned to my wife that immediately after Steve finished his game, I would drive down to Chicago to pick up Michelle . . . and maybe try to catch an inning or two of the Sox game that night.

Some people may remember that just a few years ago, the gates at ball-parks would open after the 5th inning had finished. People would line-up for the gates to open and as fans filed out, new ones walked in – free! Plus, when you drove to the park, parking was free, too, after a certain time. My dad would be proud of me for all the games we saw this way both in Milwaukee at County Stadium and at Comiskey.

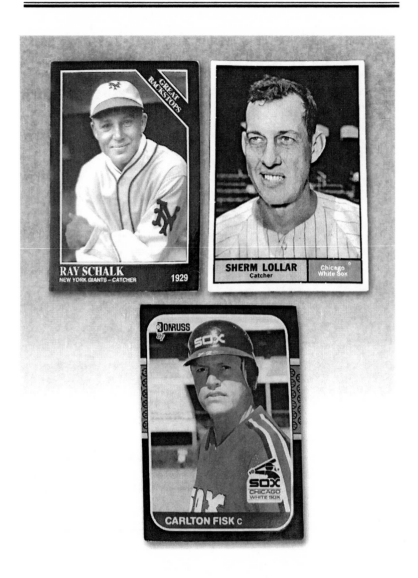

Great Chisox backstops! (L-R) Admitted into the Hall of Fame in 1955, Ray Schalk (White Sox catcher, 1912-1928) played on the 1917 World Series championship team and the 1919 American League pennant club; Sherman Lollar (White Sox catcher, 1952-1963) played on the 1959 White Sox American League pennant winner; and Carlton "Pudge" Fisk (White Sox catcher, 1981-1993), who was admitted into the Hall of Fame in 2000. Fisk played thirteen of his twenty-four seasons on the South Side.

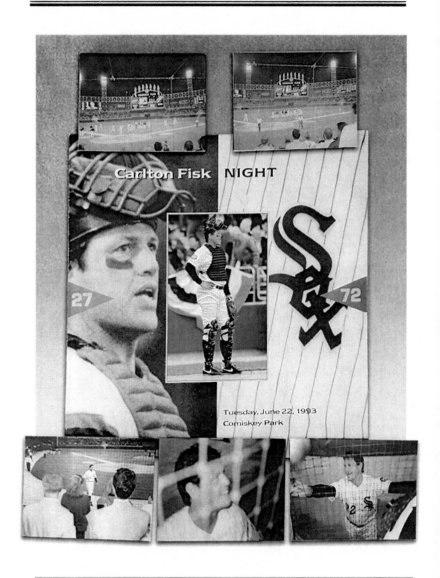

Mark was in the stands on Tuesday, June 22, 1993 when Carlton "Pudge" Fisk broke the record for number of games catching (2,226). Mark even had the chance to personally congratulate Fisk with a handshake through the backstop netting behind the plate. How nice of "Pudge" to take a moment to thank his fans following a thrilling ninth inning 3-2 victory over the Texas Rangers! In 1993, the White Sox went on to win the American League West Division with a record of 94-68.

After a fairly uneventful drive to Chicago, I got to the ballpark around 9:30 p.m. I parked – free – and as usual, walked into the park, again – free. I hustled up the ramps because I wanted to not only see the end of the game, but also to see if any Fisk souvenirs had been handed-out to mark his historic game catching record. There was! Yes, I had to pick up one of the souvenirs detailing Fisk's many achievements from the concrete floor, but I managed to find two that were fresh as new. A few days later, I gave one to my brother, Don, and kept one for myself. It still remains as one of my favorite baseball keepsakes.

I moved closer and closer to the action and eventually found myself seated in the box seats right behind the plate. The Sox rallied to win the game in the bottom of the ninth 3-2 and all of the fans were standing, cheering, and singing, "Na Na Na Na, Na Na Na Na, Hey, Hey, Goodbye!" as the scoreboard exploded fireworks in celebration. This was a magical night!

However, the evening was far from over. Not by a long-shot!

Who should emerge from the Sox dugout, but Carlton Fisk! To the delight of his adoring fans, "Pudge" began waving to the fans while he walked closer and closer to the home plate area. Would he make it to the screen behind the plate where I was now standing? Believe it or not, number 72 continued walking and waving toward the area where I was. He began shaking hands with people through the screen and guess what? I was able to be one of the lucky fans who had the opportunity to say, "Great game, 'Pudge!' Great career, 'Pudge!'" We looked at each other and he and I shook hands through the screen. What an experience!

On this historic night, everything had fallen into place. I got the chance to see our son play baseball and I shook hands with eventual Hall of Famer, Carlton Fisk! I was on cloud nine as I left Comiskey Park and drove to my wife's parents' home to pick up our daughter, Michelle. This was a night to remember!

By the way, as Stephen grew older, he became a pretty good ballplayer himself. Guess what his favorite position was? Catcher!

"Grab some bench."

"You can put it on the board! Yes! Yes!

"You gotta be bleepin' me!"

"Dadgummit!"

"He gone!"

"Stretch!"

"Mercy!"

"Can of corn."

"Duck snorts."

"Sit back. Relax and strap it down."

"The first rule of baseball is catch the baseball and the second rule is don't mess with Joe West."

"Call your sons! Call your daughters! Call your friends! Call your neighbors! Mark Buehrle has a perfect game going into the ninth!"

—Ken Harrelson

"Hawk" Harrelson has broadcast White Sox games from 1982-1985 and 1990-present. Harrelson enjoyed a nine-year Big League career playing for the Kansas City Athletics, Washington Senators, Boston Red Sox, and Cleveland Indians. In 1968, Harrelson hammered 35 home runs and knocked in 109 runs for the Red Sox leading to his selection to the American League All-Star team.

Chapter Nine

Hope Springs Eternal!

With every baseball season, a fan's hopes and dreams are filled with promise. I had the good fortune to have had many seasons of hopes and dreams as I have followed my favorite team throughout my life. Baseball is more than just a passing fancy. For kids growing up, baseball provides a rite of passage from childhood to adulthood. Baseball provides a bond between a parent and child. Memories are made in the backyard, playground, or baseball diamond with simple games of catch or watching a youngster grow in their ability to throw, catch, or hit the ball. To listen or watch a game on a warm summer evening brings joy to the fan who loves the game he grew up enjoying and playing. In many ways, baseball can keep a person forever young.

The Chicago White Sox – my team – has provided me with tremendous memories. Some of these have been written about in this book. At the same time, I hope readers will take a moment to think about their own connection with the great game of baseball.

2017 provides baseball fans – especially White Sox fans – the opportunity to look back one hundred years to the 1917 White Sox team that remains one of the greatest teams that ever took to the diamond. The team consisted of some of the finest players baseball had to offer not only during their era, but also for all-time. Plus, the intervening century of baseball on the South Side has provided fans the chance to enjoy some wonderful players – many of whom have been chronicled in this book. The author hopes that you will think about your own fan favorites, including the many exciting games you have listened to or watched over your lifetime.

I hope you have enjoyed taking a stroll down memory lane as far as the 1917 World Champion Chicago White Sox team and the many teams that have played on Chicago's South Side since.

But, a book of this kind would be remiss if it didn't take a moment to reflect on another great White Sox team. The 2005 World Series team that broke an eighty-eight year drought from 1917 to 2005. It is only deserving that the final recollection of my love affair with the White Sox highlights the 2005 World Series Chicago team!

As each baseball season draws near, fans become excited over the prospects of their team's chances to "win it all." For White Sox fans, the 2005 season brought not only expectations as the first pitch of the season was thrown, but also exhilaration when the final putout was made in the sweep of the Houston Astros in the 2005 World Series.

It's impossible for one's team to win every game or championship every year. But, the 2005 Chicago White Sox team will forever remain in the minds of White Sox fans as the team that broke the string of frustrating seasons. While embracing the memories of 2005, I hope you will also remember the 1917 White Sox team. They were a fabulous group of players!

"Get a breadth of knowledge about other stuff - know a little about a lot."

"Meeting friends for dinner. Went to type 'I am seated in a booth' and nearly sent 'I am sedated in a booth.' Different story."

"You can either call it forgetting to turn in a hotel room key or gaining a book mark."

"I am thankful for the scores of new @whitesox friends I made this year. Ya'll are the best. That includes you, @stevestone."

Jason Benetti

Hired in 2016, Benetti is the newest member of the White Sox broadcasting team. His knowledge of the game, coupled with his unusual humor, brings a fresh look and sound to broadcasts.

9th Inning

2005 – A Magical Season To Remember!

My father never lived to see the White Sox win a World Series. "Big Ed" Pienkos was born in 1920 and died in 1999. Although he watched and listened on his transistor radio to many baseball games in his life, he never saw the Sox win the World Series.

But, I have!

Do you remember the exact date as to when the White Sox won the 2005 World Series? Before I review the White Sox post-season that led to a World Series, its first in 88 years on the South Side, I'd like to mention how numbers have been a part of my life. Maybe yours, too?

I've always had a knack for remembering important dates, anniversaries, birthdays, anything that has to do with numbers. Even baseball players uniform numbers. For instance, I can remember the opening day starters and their uniform numbers for the 1959 White Sox. Can you? There's Little Louie Aparicio leading off and wearing number 11 playing shortstop. Nelson Fox bats second, plays second base and wears number 2 on the back of his uniform. Batting third and playing centerfield is number 1 Jim Landis followed by the remainder of the starters: Earl Torgeson who plays first base and wears number 17. Playing left field is number 16 Al Smith. In rightfield is Jim McAnany wearing number 3. Behind the plate is number 10 Sherman Lollar. Starting pitchers for the Sox in 1959 are Barry Latman (#18), Billy Pierce (#19), Dick

Donavan (#22), and Early Wynn (#24). In the bullpen are two steady relievers, Gerry Staley (#21) and Turk Lown (#27). Besides Sox players, I can remember many others, especially when I was growing up and followed teams on a daily basis. Guys like Roberto Clemente (#21), Mickey Mantle (#7), Ted Williams (#9), Hank Aaron (#44), Willie Mays (#24), Yogi Berra (#8), Roger Maris (#9), and I could go on and on about players on opposing teams. I'm sure lots of kids growing up could do the same. I just seemed to remember players by remembering their uniform numbers. Like my favorite White Sox players: Mike Hershberger (#40), Ray Herbert (#21), Bill Melton (#14), Pete Ward (#8), and so on. The players in the 50s and 60s when I was growing up stick in my mind more than those in more recent years because players tended to stick with a club for most of their careers. Today with free agency, players move around a lot more than they did in the "old days."

The 2005 season was going to be a magical one. The Sox put together a team that withstood all the adventures a team needs to face during the long, long baseball season. Led by first baseman Paul Konerko, second baseman Tadahito Iguchi, shortstop Juan Uribe, third baseman Joe Crede, left-fielder Scott Podsednik, centerfielder Aaron Rowand, rightfielder (and World Series MVP) Jermaine Dye, and catcher A.J. Pierzynski, plus the excellent season pitched by Jon Garland (18-10), Mark Buehrle (16-8), Jose Contreras (15-7), Freddie Garcia (14-8), and Orlando Hernandez (9-9), the Sox cruised through the 2005 season winning 99 games and losing 63. A late season swoon saw their division lead dwindle until the ship was righted and the Sox took the division crown by six games over the second place Cleveland Indians. Manager Ozzie Guillen and General Manager Kenny Williams were about to orchestrate something that hadn't happened since 1917 in Chicago: Win the World Series!

The White Sox opened the playoffs at home against the Wild Card entry Boston Red Sox in the American League Division Series.

Although the White Sox would sweep Boston 3-0, the teams battled in what was one of the tensest series of the post-season. The White Sox won the first game handily behind the superb pitching of Contreras, 14-2 (reminiscent of Game 1 of the 1959 World Series when the White Sox walloped the Los Angeles Dodgers at Old Comiskey Park, 11-0). Buehrle took to the hill for Game 2 that saw the White Sox come back from a four run deficit to score five runs in the fifth inning that held up in a 5-4 victory. Chicago was one game away from taking on the winner of the other three game series between the New York Yankees and Los Angeles Angels.

Game 3 was one to remember. At Fenway Park, in the sixth inning of a 2-2 tie game, Paul Konerko hit a two-run homer to put the Sox ahead, 4-2. The Red Sox scored a run in the bottom of the inning and then proceeded to load the bases. Orlando Hernández (known as "El Duque"), came in to pitch with no outs. Hernandez got the first batter he faced to foul out, and the second batter to pop out to short. El Duque went to a full count before striking out Johnny Damon to end the inning without giving up another run. Hernandez pitched three innings in relief, giving up just one hit. Bobby Jenks closed the game, earning his second save of the series. The victory over the Red Sox was the first postseason series win by the White Sox since the 1917 World Series, which was the last time they won the World Series.

The Sox opened the American League Championship Series at home against the Los Angeles Angels who had defeated the New York Yankees three games to two in their series. If the White Sox-Red Sox series was tense, the White Sox-Angels series was weird. Even though the White Sox would win the series four games to one, one game stands out as to why this had to be the Sox year.

In Game 1, the White Sox had the chance to rest while waiting to see who they would play as the Yankees and Angels battled in their five game series. *Jose Contreras pitched extremely well going 8⅓ innings. But he took the loss, his first since August 15ᵗʰ, as Los Angeles won 3-2.*

Game 2 was a game to remember. Mark Buehrle pitched an outstanding five-hit game through nine innings and was ready to take to the mound in the tenth if the 1-1 tie was not broken in the Sox at-bat. The Sox did score in their bottom half of the ninth, but it was the manner in which they scored the winning run that will always be remembered by Sox fans that were at the game or watched the game on T.V., listened to it on the radio, or read about in the newspaper.

Mark's snapshots around 35ᵗʰ and Shields (the crossroads of White Sox baseball) during the White Sox 2005 World Series run. Chicago hometown pride at its finest! Besides photos, a replica World Series ring (given to fans in 2015 on the tenth anniversary of 2005 team) the official World Series cap, and a baseball autographed by right fielder Jermaine Dye, 2005 World Series Most Valuable Player.

What happened was weird.

With two outs, A.J. Pierzynski appeared to swing and miss as he struck out against reliever Kelvim Escobar who had been mowing down Sox hitters in his three innings of relief. But, did A.J. strike out to end the inning and force the two teams to go into extra innings?

Replays showed the home plate umpire signaling that A.J. had indeed struck out.

Pierzynski had taken a few steps back towards the Sox dugout, but he alertly realized that he had not heard the home plate umpire call him out. Pierzynski took off for first base. The Angels' catcher, ex-White Sox Josh Paul, thinking the inning was over, rolled the ball back to the mound. Pierzynski was ruled safe at first. Pinch runner Pablo Ozuna promptly stole second and then scored on Joe Crede's double off the left field wall. Sox win! Who knows what would have happened had the game gone into extra innings? But this alert move by Pierzynski, and the run that was scored in the bottom of the ninth, may have been the springboard needed for this Sox team to not only win the American League Championship Series, but also the 2005 World Series.

The Sox won the next three games and took the series, and their first American League pennant since 1959, four games to one over the Angels.

The four consecutive complete games in a postseason by Sox pitchers (Buehrle, Garland, Garcia, and Contreras) were a League Championship Series record. It was the first time since the Yankees had five complete games in a row pitched by Whitey Ford, Tom Sturdivant, Don Larsen (a perfect game), Bob Turley, and Johnny Kucks as New York won the World Series against the Brooklyn Dodgers in 1956.

The White Sox were playing in their first World Series since 1959. Their opponents were the Houston Astros who had defeated the St. Louis Cardinals to make their first trip to the World Series. It was a brief one! The Sox swept the Astros four game to none.

Highlights of the Series were many: In Game 1, Bobby Jenks getting one of his two Series saves (four overall after earning two in the Boston series) in a 5-3 Sox victory. Paul Konerko hitting a grand slam in the seventh inning of Game 2, erasing a 4-2 deficit. Then in the same game, Scott Podsednik hit a walk-off home run in the bottom of the ninth to win the game for the Sox, 7-6. Game 3 was the longest game in World Series history as far as time goes, and the extra-inning affair tied for the longest in World Series history. The Sox won in fourteen innings, 7-5, as Mark Buehrle came in from the bullpen to earn the save. The Sox swept the Series winning Game 4 by the score of 1-0. World Series MVP Jermaine Dye hit an RBI single in the eighth inning and Bobby Jenks earned the save for the Sox to win the World Championship. However, the defensive heroics of shortstop Juan Uribe should not be overlooked as Uribe made two sensational defensive plays in the bottom of the ninth to prevent the Astros from possibly winning the game. He dove into the stands to make a catch of a foul ball which is one of the greatest catches in the history of the World Series. Uribe then threw out Orlando Palmeiro to end the game as he raced behind the mound on a slowly hit ball that went over the head of reliever Jenks.

The Chicago White Sox had won the World Series! Their first since 1917! And here's where dates and numbers come into play and why I won't forget when the Sox won their 2005 World Series Championship. The date was October 26th, my wife, Ann's, birthday. We didn't celebrate her big day until the final out was recorded. And, I won't ever forget to remember her birthday in the future because I'll never forget when the White Sox won the World Series!

By the way, the White Sox 11-1 post season record tied the 1999 New York Yankees for the best record in a single post-season.

Somewhere in heaven I knew my Dad was smiling. I was!

Mark's Frank Thomas memorabilia. "The Big Hurt" is the greatest offensive player in White Sox history. Number 35 played sixteen of his nineteen-year Big League career on the South Side. He was the American League Most Valuable Player in consecutive seasons, 1993 and 1994. Thomas was a five-time All-Star. No other player in baseball history – not Babe Ruth, Lou Gehrig, or Ted Williams – had seven consecutive seasons of at least 20 home runs, 100 RBI, 100 walks, and a batting average over .300. His career numbers: .301 Batting Average, 521 Home Runs, and 1,704, Runs Batted In. In 2014, "The Big Hurt" was elected to the Hall of Fame in his first year of eligibility.

"That certainly was a highlight of my career. It was a magical year because we were in first place the whole season. One of the most memorable things was the parade, everybody turning out. It was all Chicago, everybody was happy for us. It was a very proud moment. I was so happy to be a part of it. We brought the organ down and it was on stage (at the rally). It was part of the pageantry."

(Speaking of the 2005 White Sox World Championship year.)

—Nancy Faust

A fan favorite, Faust was the ballpark organist for the White Sox from 1970-2010.

Stella and Edward Pienkos Educational Fund

As mentioned earlier, a portion of the proceeds from this book goes into the Stella and Edward Pienkos Educational Fund. My parents, especially my mother, preached getting a solid education to her three sons. They listened. Even though my mother never attended high school – in fact, she began working in 8ᵗʰ grade so she was not able to participate in her school's graduation ceremony – and my father only went one year to high school, they knew the importance of education. As countless children heard many times from their Great Depression parents while growing up: "Education is something they can't take away from you."

In memory of my parents, my wife and I have established a scholarship fund to assist high school students in their desire "to get an education." This is one way of saying "Thank You" to my parents for all they did for us, plus a way of "paying it forward" to help other young people reach their future goals.

I certainly hope you enjoyed reading this book. It's my way of saying "Thank You" to the Chicago White Sox for being such a positive influence not only in my life, but also in my family's. I know other Sox fans feel the same.

The current White Sox owner, Mr. Jerry Reinsdorf, deserves a great deal of credit for the ball club taking the field each season in what is now called Guaranteed Rate Field. He has continued the legacy of great White Sox owners. Also, Mr. Reinsdorf will always be remembered as the owner of an organization who brought joy to so many people as the White Sox achieved a World Series title in 2005!

If you have a high school son or daughter, or a grandchild that is graduating high school this year, or you know someone who could benefit by being considered for this scholarship, please have them complete the scholarship application form.

Thank you for taking the time to read this book. Also, thank you for mentioning this scholarship opportunity to someone who will use it in the way it was intended: To get a solid education!

Stella and Edward Pienkos Educational Fund Scholarship
Submission deadline is April 15ˢᵗ of each year

Student's Name _____

Student's Address _____

_____

_____

Year Graduating from High School _____

Name and location of High School _____

_____

_____

_____

Technical College/College/University planning to attend in the Fall

_____

_____

Intended Major _____

Why I would like to be a recipient of the Stella and Edward
Pienkos Educational Fund Scholarship: _____

_____

_____

Recipients will be notified of their selection no later than July 15ᵗʰ
each year. Please mail to:

Stella and Edward Pienkos Educational Fund
To print an application, please go to markpienkos.com
Mailing instructions are on the form —
Thank You and Best Wishes!

PLAY BALL!

Chicago White Sox Chairman Jerry Reinsdorf (holding trophy) is surrounded by members of the 2005 team as they gathered on July 18, 2015 to celebrate the tenth anniversary of the White Sox winning the World Series. To Mr. Reinsdorf's right are: Executive Vice President Kenny Williams and Manager Ozzie Guillen (Number 13).

Chicago White Sox Charities

Mark wanted to join other White Sox fans in inscribing their names and favorite memories at U.S. Cellular Field (formerly Comiskey Park, now Guaranteed Rate Field) as part of a diamond-shaped brick plaza and commemorative monument. It is the focal point of the ballpark's main entrance. At the very heart of the new plaza is a dramatic bronze and granite sculpture celebrating the franchise's 2005 World Series Championship.

Mark and son, Steve, were present at the dedication ceremonies of the plaza on Saturday, July 18, 2015 during the 10th anniversary of the White Sox World Series run. On hand were 33,559 loyal fans to see the Sox take on the Kansas City Royals. Unfortunately, the Sox lost 7-6 in an exciting thirteen inning contest. One consolation, the first twenty thousand fans in attendance received a commemorative 2005 World Series ring. Priceless!

Proceeds from brick sales went to support Chicago White Sox Charities. Since 1991, Chicago White Sox Charities has donated millions of dollars to cancer research and treatment, youth education and athletics, and programs that support Chicago kids and families.

About the Author

Born in Chicago in 1950, Mark's family moved from the Riverview Amusement Park area to the South Side in 1955. He grew up playing lots of sports, especially baseball, resulting in a life-long passion for the White Sox.

Mark graduated from St. Laurence High School in 1968 and went on to earn degrees from Northern Illinois University (B.S.Ed., M.S.Ed.), the University of Wisconsin-Milwaukee (Specialist Certificate in Administrative Leadership), and the University of Southern California (Doctorate in Education).

A professional educator, Mark has enjoyed an outstanding 44-year career that incudes teaching, school counselor, associate

principal, principal, and superintendent. He has also taught graduate level courses in Florida and Wisconsin.

Besides sports, Mark's other interests include reading, travel, enjoying family & friends, and community involvement. The latter has found Mark being elected twice as alderman in Muskego, WI, appointed to the Police & Fire Commission in Lake Geneva, WI serving as president for three of his five-year term, and being active in local, state, and national politics. Mark served as president of the Wisconsin School Counselors Association and Midwest Vice President for the American School Counselor Association. He is active in several Polish American organizations serving as state division president for the Polish American Congress and currently serves as vice president for public relations for the national PAC. In 2015, Mark was honored by the President of Poland receiving the Cavalier's Cross of the Order of Merit of the Republic of Poland for his efforts to bring greater understanding between the U.S. and Poland. Mark also is a 4th Degree Knight of Columbus.

Mark married Ann (Lesniewski) in 1972. Ann immigrated to the U.S. from Poland in 1959. An avid photographer and family book creator, Ann has returned to her country of birth over 25 times. They have three great adult children, Michelle, Karen, and Stephen, two wonderful sons-in-laws, Alex and Matt, plus three lovely grandchildren, Estelle, Amy, and Nathan. More than enough to field a baseball team!

GO WHITE SOX!

CPSIA information can be obtained
at www.ICGtesting.com
Printed in the USA
LVOW12*2242090517
533837LV00004B/5/P